THE NEW WOMAN
IN INDIAN ENGLISH FICTION

A Study of Kamala Markandaya, Anita Desai, Namita Gokhale & Shobha De

CREATIVE NEW LITERATURES SERIES-14

THE NEW WOMAN IN INDIAN ENGLISH FICTION

A STUDY OF KAMALA MARKANDAYA,
ANITA DESAI, NAMITA GOKHALE & SHOBHA DE

SHARAD SRIVASTAVA

CREATIVE BOOKS
NEW DELHI

Published by :
CREATIVE BOOKS
CB-24, Ring Road, Naraina, New Delhi-110 028
Ph : 329 8487

© Reserved with the Author

First Edition : 1996
ISBN 81-86318-36-4

Typesetting by :
MOGHA PRINTERS
RZE-11, Gandhi Market, West Sagar Pur,
New Delhi-110 046
Ph. : 550 3175

Printed at:
NICE PRINTERS
Delhi

Contents

Preface
vii

Introduction
1

Feminism And Feminist Movements
6

Anticipating The 'New Woman' : Kamala Markandaya
24

The 'New Woman' Proper : Anita Desai
48

The 'Aberration'-I : Shobha De
81

The 'Aberration'-II : Namita Gokhale
101

Conclusion
119

Bibliography
132

Index
138

Dedicated

to

Prof. S. N. Joshi

PREFACE

The present investigation began as a study of the women characters of four women authors, Kamala Markandaya, Anita Desai, Namita Gokhale and Shobha De. At that time only one novel *Paro* of Namita Gokhale and four novels of Shobha De had been published. Namita Gokhale's *Gods, Graves and Grand Mother* Shobha De's *Sultry Days* appeared during the course of this study. As the study progressed, I discovered something distinct in the women characters of Kamala Markandaya and Anita Desai - something in their spiritual and emotional make-up which was trying to express itself in their attitude to persons and events. I saw in these characters an urge to seek self-fulfillment through self-expression. This urge, at times, was codified as 'metaphors'. Further investigation suggested to me that these characters showed as distinct pattern of evolution. What was at the level of awareness in Kamala Markandaya's novels became clearly identifiable in the novels of Anita Desai.

But when I came to the novels of Namita Gokhale and Shobha De it was apparent that their women characters did not fit into this pattern of development. But the characters of Kamala Markandaya and Anita Desai had made so deep an impression in my mind that I remained firm in my belief that the development of women characters in serious mainstream fiction must be along the lines of achieving self-fulfillment through self-expression and not along self-assertion and dominance. The women characters of Namita Gokhale and Shobha De could only be regarded sallies or aberrations and the serious novelist must at some point return to this mainstream. This belief got support from the novel *Sultry Days* of Shobha De, where Pramila after her period of such sallies finally return to her roots. This aberrant behaviour aimed at dominance is only at the periphery while at the core a woman always possesses the urge to seek self-fulfillment through self expression. This, I decided to call the 'new woman' which is different from the so called emancipated, economically independent self-asserting modern woman. So I came to the conclusion that in Kamla Makandaya we find the 'new woman' in making; in Anita Desai, the 'new woman' proper emerges and in Namita Gokhale and Shobha De the women make a sudden and brief sally away from the mainstream. But there is always the urge at the core to return to the mainstream. I have also tried to suggest that even in the future the development of the 'new woman' in novels will be along this mainstream; and if there are such occasional sallies away from it, they will finally return to the mainstream.

The study of feminism and feminist movement was done at a much later stage of the investigation mainly to test the ideas that had been taking shape in my mind. I discovered that there too, serious feminist theories are concerned with basic issues. But there also one often comes across such views which might be labelled as aberrations. I have called such views 'the Paradox of Feminism'.

Throughout the course of my study I have kept in mind that my field is literature. So I have scrupulously avoided the sociological approach to the problem of the 'new woman'. Hence, the argument of my approach is almost independent of the chapter on feminism.

SHARAD SRIVASTAVA

1

INTRODUCTION

The emergence of the 'new woman' is a global phenomenon. So also are the stresses and strains she faces the world over. The discrimination she has to face, the sense of insecurity which she feels, the sexual harassment and violence to which she is exposed are similar in the advanced as well as in the developing countries. The other traits of the 'new woman' also have a universal character such as her determination to oppose sexual harassment and male-domination, the urge to create a milieu for the full expression of her emotional and moral self and what is most important to her — the craving to be accepted as an individual, a person in her own right and enjoying the same status as man has always enjoyed.

In this pseudo-moral system of male-dominated society a woman has been the victim of male-hypocrisy, exploitation and violence since the earliest times but she could not freely narrate or openly discuss these experiences. Women have also, since the earliest times, entered into intimate relationships with men both of a physical and spiritual nature but they could not talk about them. With the emergence of the feminist movement in the west, the emancipated women started freely discussing such experiences in their autobiographies. In India also, women authors have boldly come out with intimate details of their lives in their autobiographies. When women could talk so freely about themselves, it was natural that they would be more uninhibited in their writings, especially in their novels. A few examples of some autobiographies of women authors would drive home the point.

Kamala Das narrates in her autobiography, *My Story* how when she got engages, her fiance "pushed me into a dark corner behind a door and kissed me sloppily near my mouth. He crushed by breasts with his thick fingers. Don't you love me, he asked me, don't you like my touching you... I felt hurt and humiliated"[1] (85). She also talks about how a neighbour, with the connivance of her maid-servant raped her[2] (113). Amrita Pritam, another well-known writer and champion of the cause of women, freely talks about her intimate relationships with different men at different times in her autobio-graphy, *Raseedi Ticket*[3] (Revenue Stamp). In a very intimate manner she describes her infatuation for Sahir Ludhianwi and a similar passion which Sajjad Zahir had for her. She also traces how the love of Imroz — a painter several years younger in age - helped her realise her own self, spiritually and emotionally. The renowned Marathi stage and film artiste, Hansa Wadkar relates how she was raped by a middle-aged magistrate of a mofussil town whom she and her husband had approached for help. The magistrate sent away her husband on some pretext and then shut the door and threatened her that if she resisted she would face terrible consequences. In this way he raped her in the court-room itself while his wife and children were all the time there in the adjacent room. She says, "...that day I knew for the first time what rape actually means"[4] (62).

These examples show the courage with which the Indian women authors reveal what a woman has to face in this male-dominated society. Autobiographies reveal the reality and these experiences are of women and they are by no means confined to these women authors alone. They more or less reveal the general lot of women. Yet an experience cannot be universalised in an autobiography. However, the necessary aesthetic distancing where we can observe this conflict and at the same time view it in its broader social perspective is only possible in a creative literary work like a novel.

The Indo-English women writers have a special advantage in this respect as they have themselves been exposed to the stresses and strains to which the 'new woman' is subjected. Also, writing in the English language is sometimes more helpful to an uninhibited frankness so necessary to the portrayal of the emotional, moral and spiritual problems of the 'new woman'. Therein lies the relevance of the present study.

It is basically a study of women characters of women novelists. The objective is to study how and to what extent these novelists through their women characters are able to project the image of the 'new woman'. At the conceptual level the 'new woman' is seen as distinct from the modern or the emancipated woman. Hence, it is possible that a woman can be a 'new woman' without herself being aware of the fact. The 'new woman' is one who has a value-system and a commitment to these values. She is painfully aware of the price she has to pay in adhering to these values in a male dominated society.

The study also seeks to discover in these women characters a continuity based on the realisation of this world view. It studies the women novelists in this light also. It shows that a thread of continuity runs through the women characters of the novelists studied. There is first the awareness of the 'new woman'; then the emergence of the 'new woman proper'. Along with these there are 'sallies' away from the mainstream development of the 'new woman' with the hints that in the end the woman has to return to the mainstream. Hence, such 'sallies' have been called "aberrations" from the mainstream. The study has been able to show that from the point of view of the 'new woman' the four novelists studied fall into an identifiable pattern. The first two of these, Kamala Markandaya and Anita Desai portray the 'new woman' of the mainstream while the other two, Shobha De and Namita Gokhale present its 'aberration.'

The 'new woman', as has been described in the theoretical chapter, is concerned with the more fundamental problems of a woman in moral, emotional and spiritual fields whereas for the women under the category 'aberrations' these problems remain at the periphery of their personalities, none of them touching the core of her being. The concerns of an 'aberration' - woman are similar to those of a modern woman. In a way, they approximate the concerns of the feminists viz. economic independence, social emancipation, acquiring an identity at par with men, etc. The study is free from this so-called feminist obsession. However, to place the study in perspective a chapter on feminism and its significant developments has been included.

There are a few critics who have written about the women writers of Indian fiction in English. N. Meena Belliappa[5] and C. Vimala Rao[6] have written about the women writers in India; they are useful and commendable in a pioneering kind of way. They indicate, however, the need for searching criticism in this area rather than fulfil it. They tend to concentrate on the gender identity of the authors in question rather than the women characters in fiction. Another critic who has attempted a full-length analysis of women novelists is Meena

Shirwadkar.[7] Her work assumes significance inasmuch as it traces the image of the woman in Indo-English writers right from pre-independence times to the seventies. Since it includes many authors, both male as well as female, her work does not make an in-depth study of its women characters.

Only one critical work which deserves special mention is of Shantha Krishnaswamy.[8] Her study directs attention on the woman's awakening consciousness and her confrontation against a male-dominated, tradition oriented society between 1950 and 1980 as reflected in the novels of six major writers: Raja Rao, R. K. Narayan, Bhabani Bhattacharya, Kamala Markandaya, Anita Dessai and Ruth Prawar Jhabhwala. Of these her views on the women characters of Kamala Markandaya and Anita Desai need to be referred here. According to Krishnaswamy, in Kamala Markandaya's novels "the quest for autonomy leads her to nurturance of warm familial relationships, which in turn progresses towards imaginative sympathy for the human race"[9]. As regards Anita Desai, Krishnaswamy considers her novels as registering a conscious rebellion against the entire system of social relationships thereby endowing Anita Desai with a streak of radical feminism. She is the first critic to discover a thematic development through a chronological order of these novels. She analyses this and describes it as a development of mental experience which has three important stages : self-delusion, fragmentation and schizophrenia and, finally, visionary intuition. Despite the in-depth analyses of women characters of Kamala Markandaya and Anita Desai, the work of Krishaswamy does not do so under a definite framework which the present study seeks to do.

The present study includes four women authors -- Kamala Markandaya, Anita Desai, Shobha De and Namita Gokhale -- whose works broadly encompass the period between 1950s and 1990s. Although there is enough critical work on Kamala Makandaya and Anita Desai, the present study is the first full-length study of its kind on Namita Gokhale and Shobha De. So far, the analyses of the fiction of these two authors have remained confined to reviews and stray articles in newspapers, magazines and journals. By studying these two new authors with the two already established ones and presenting all of them through an integrated approach, the study attempts to work in a direction hitherto untouched in the field of Indo-English fiction. Also, by analysing Namita Gokhale's latest work, *Gods, Graves and Grand-*

mother in the light of the eighteenth century novelist, Daniel Defoe's famous work, *Moll Flanders*, it opens a new way of approaching women characters in modern fiction.

NOTES

1. Kamala Das, *My Story* (New Delhi : Sterling Publishers, 1977) 85.
2. Das 113.
3. Amrita Pritam, *Raseedi Ticket* (New Delhi : Kitabghar, 1993).
4. Hansa Wadkar, *Sangtye Aika* (Pune : Rajhans Prakashak, 1993) 62. Since the original text is in Marathi, the quote has been translated in English.
5. N. Meena Belliappa, "East West Encounter : Indian Women Writers of Fiction in English," *Fiction and the Reading Public in India* ed. C. D. Narasimaiah (Mysore : University Press of Mysore, 1967) 18-27.
6. C. Vimala Rao, "The Achievement of the Indian Women Novelists," *Indian Literature of the Past-Fifty Years (1917 - 1967)* ed. C. D. Narasimaiah (Mysore : University of Mysore, 1970) 213-224.
7. Meena Shirwadker, *Image of Woman in the Indo-Anglian Novel* (New Delhi : Sterling Publishers, 1979).
8. Shantha Krishnaswamy, *The Woman in Indian Fiction in English* (New Delhi : Ashish Publishing House, 1984).
9. Kishnaswamy vi.

2

FEMINISM AND FEMINIST MOVEMENTS

The impact of the significant economic and social movements is also seen in the literature of every age. But literature is primarily a creative art and economic and sociological movements can appear in literature only in so far as they are governed and transformed by the laws of the creative art. This is also true when we come to the feminist movement and its expression in literature. It would not, therefore, be valid to study a literary work as a projection of a social movement. Yet a knowledge of the movement is helpful to an appreciation of that literary work. Feminism as a movement has been well established. Women creative artists especially women novelists cannot remain untouched by this movement. This is all the more so when such novelists are themselves emancipated women who are well familiar with this movement. Hence, a survey of feminism will be helpful to an understanding of the novelists under study.

The theory of feminism and its influence have spread so rapidly in the latter half of this century that it is now almost impossible to define it in a few words. Contemporary feminist thought has branched and spread into such a wide variety of approaches and attitudes pertaining to the question of women. Alix Kates Shulman observes :

Feminism is not a monolith : there are many different, even at times contradictory positions which may spring from good feminist motives[1] (32-33).

The current concerns of feminism extend from the overt oppression that male-dominated social order imposes on an uneducated and financially backward or conventionally religious woman to the invisible and subtle strain experienced by the educated and seemingly independent women in the so called civilized and developed societies.

What is now popularly known as modern feminism or the second phase of women's movement is the world wide awareness of the oppression of women and subsequent protest triggered by the early writings of Simone de Beauvoir, Betty Friedan, Germain Greer and others. Yet this second phase of feminist consciousness is inevitably linked with the earlier women's movement -- the suffragette movement -- of the previous century, which earned the women equal political and legal rights. A quick look at the intellectual revolutions that resulted in the origin and development of this earlier women's movement may provide us with some insight into some of the most important concerns that continue to engage modern feminist thought.

In the West three intellectual revolutions of the past have played significant roles in moulding the structure of feminist thought. The oldest of these is the birth of liberalism in the seventeenth and eighteenth centuries. The important concern of this theory was the "rights of man", expressed mainly through the writings of Locke, Rousseau and others. These writings later formed the basis of the explicit democratic goals of the French and American revolutions. Contesting the divine right of monarchs and aristocrats to political rule, the liberal theory legitimised the political participation of all male members though initially it restricted these to the propertied classes. Liberalism was essentially concerned with the rights of the citizens before the law and to participate in public life, especially to vote. These ideas were almost immediately followed by subsequent equivalent claims about "the rights of women" to participate in public life and to vote, to hold political office and own property.

The feminist theories, which although originated in the West, are valid for all societies. These are the socialist theories especially those of Marx and Engels. The Marxist-socialist theory grew from the realisation that political liberalism was hollow without economic equality. Thus the economic right, that is, the right to economic equality was added to political ones. Feminists, influenced by the Marxist theories, later came to be called Socialist Feminists.

The third important stream of thought that has considerably influenced modern feminism is the late nineteenth century and early twentieth century examination of sexuality and sexual behaviour in its social and political contexts caused by the tremendous developments in the field of psychology and the devastating change in perspective that followed it. Freud, Jung and later Lacan played roles of tremendous significance in channelling modern feminist thought to unexplored new regions. The novel insights offered by these new psychological theories resulted in a widespread rethinking on the relationship of sexuality to society. It also revived the interest to know more about the relation of repression to civilization and of the individual psychic formation to the creation and reproduction of social order. Expressions like 'sex role stereotyping' soon became frequently used expressions in feminist writings.

While the prominent concern of the first phase of feminist movement was the political rights of woman, its second phase has as its concern the cultural, socio - political, economic and even psychic and spiritual aspects of women's liberation. Poised against the overt and covert oppressive strains exerted on women by the male-dominated social machinery, this second coming of feminism is noted for its multi-dimensional perspective and devastating attack on several age-old conventions of social formation. To put it briefly, we can say that this second phase of feminism has an essential deconstructive nature.

There are many senses in which the sprawling edifice of modern feminism can be considered as built on the foundations laid by Simone de Beauvoir in *The Second Sex* (1949). Beauvoir's analysis of women's subordination proceeded from the assumption that men viewed women as fundamentally different from themselves. In being defined as 'the other', women were reduced to the status of 'The second sex.' The masculine is accepted as the norm. Humanity is male and woman is defined not in herself but as relative to man, never as an autonomous being. She is the incidental, inessential as opposed to the essential or the basic. Many of the best known writings of this second wave could be seen as a set of variations on this theme. Germaine Greer discusses how the restrictions imposed on their emotions and sexual instincts reduce women to Female Eunuchs. Betty Freidan calls attention to the 'problem that has no name' experienced by the 'happily' married housewives and reveals how the conventionally assigned role results in the construction of a female mystique.

Among various other factors, an important reason that motivated this second flowering of feminism was the profound anti-feminist attitude that prevailed after the World War. Once the war was over, women who had, in the absence of men, been responsible for many functions in public life were coerced into returning to a domestic life. A virtual cultural blitz emphasized the crucial importance of full time mothers and wives. The contradictions did not go unnoticed. One of the important contributions of the upsurge of the second phase of women's movement to universal feminist consciousness is the awareness of the 'patriarchal' nature of human societies.

The word 'patriarchy', with its roots in the Greek *patros* was introduced by Kate Millet in *Sexual Politics* (1970) to refer to male-dominated power structure that forms the basis of our society. Millet elaborated on how the power of 'patriarchy' is maintained even in modern societies where women have education, access to financial resources and extensive civil and political rights. This is accomplished mainly by means of an ideological engineering of consent among women themselves. Thus, the picture of women's oppression that emerges from Millet's analysis is essentially that of an interior colonization. The women are socially conditioned to embrace their secondary status. According to Millet, in modern times patriarchy is upheld chiefly by attitudes rather than political or economic structures. This patriarchy is so deeply ingrained into our thinking that the character structure it creates in both the sexes is more a habit of mind and a way of life than a political system[2] (60).

Early feminist theorists like Simone de Beauvoir and others gave great importance to the issue of women's experience. They believed that women's experience was different from that of men because of their long oppression. But in the seventies there took place a paradoxical shift in the terms of the debate. The exponents of this new changed perspective refused to consider women's difference from men as a form of inadequacy and a source of pride and confidence. Some of them went to the extent of advocating to establish femaleness as normative and maleness as a derivation of it, thereby attempting a direct reversal of the Freudian perspective. The mother-centred theories of Jacques Lacan and the entry of lesbian feminists into the field of active theorizing led this change in perspective to new horizons. The significant theorists of modern feminism have now engaged themselves in several well-defined groups such as Marxist-socialist-feminists, radical and lesbian feminists, liberal feminists, etc.. Despite divergence in their perspective, they are united by a common belief that women are oppressed—culturally, politically and psychologically and exploited economically. Further, that this system is maintained and reproduced by a patriarchal structure that seeks to naturalize it. The discussion that follows will sketch the ideas guiding each of the three groups at present.

Having a rich tradition of western socialism to draw upon, socialist feminist ideology is the most elaborate of the three. Marx and Engels have considered the status of women in the family and in the society from an entirely new angle. In the *Communist Manifesto* (1848) the bourgeois attitude to woman has been exposed. Engels, in his long essay, 'The Origin of Family, Private Property and State', examines the change in the status of women from the barbarian society to the modern bourgeois society. He sums up his own view and also that of Karl Marx on the entire man-women relationship in one sentence :

The first class antagonism which appears in history coincides with the development of antagonism between man and woman in monogamian marriage, and the first class oppression with that of female sex by the male[3] (495).

He ridicules the idea of monogamy because in the male-dominated society 'monogamy (is) *only for the* woman'. *Communist Manifesto* says :

Our bourgeois, not content with having the wives and daughters of their proletarians at their disposal, not to speak of common prostitutes, take the greatest pleasure in seducing each other's wives[4] (50).

This notion of bourgeois marriage and chastity for women has distorted the image of woman in literature. It has given rise to two characters in bourgeois literature — 'the wife's paramour and the cuckold'. The bourgeois marriage reduces the wife to the level of the prostitute. Marx and Engels believed that a woman can never find her status based on dignity and freedom in a bourgeois society. It is only in a communist society that the woman would be really free and her dignity would be restored to her. Marx says, "If a marriage based on love is moral then a marriage is moral only till love lasts."(508).

In the bourgeois society woman will always remain suppressed. Man will have all the privileges while woman none. This follows from the very nature of the bourgeois society. No reform movement aiming at improving the condition of women can alter the status of woman in a bourgeois society. It is only in a communist society that woman will have dignity and will be able to find self-fulfilment.

What, then, is the socialist feminist vision of society after the revolution? No one has drawn the blue prints, but the general outlines are clear. The society would be democratic, both politically and economically. The means of production would be publicly owned and the fruits of production equally distributed. Factors like sex and race would no longer pre-determine one's status of life style. Most of the functions that the family now performs — child care, for example — would be socially performed and as a result, the oppressiveness of the present bourgeois family would cease. According to Juliet Mitchell, an important advocate of modern socialist feminism, the result would be, not the destruction of the family, but "a plural range of institutions — where the family is only one ....."[5] (123).

Differing significantly from this view, the radical feminists believe that the oppression of women is the first and most basic case of domination by one group over another. "Male supremacy is the oldest, most basic form of domination. All other forms of exploitation and oppression (racism, capitalism, imperialism, etc.) are extensions of male supremacy : Men dominate women and few men dominate the rest"[6] (Betty and Roszak 273).

Among radical feminists only Shulamith Firestone has developed a comprehensive theory of the origins of women's oppression. The origins of sex class system, she says, lie in the biologically determined reproductive roles of men and women : women bear and nurse children, "unlike economic class, sex class sprang directly from a biological reality : men and women were created different and equally privileged"[7] (8). Until reliable birth control methods became available, women were " at the continual mercy of their biology"[8] (Firestone 8). Biology made women dependent on males for the physical survival. Thus "the biological family is an inherently unequal power distribution (Firestone 8). The result is power psychology and the economic class system. "Natural reproductive differences between the sexes led directly to the first division of labour at the origins of class"[10] (Firestone 9).

Although women's oppression has its origins in biology, it is not therefore, immutable. Technological developments — reliable birth control, and in future, artificial reproduction (i.e test-tube babies) — have the potential of freeing women. Thus, according to Firestone, revolution is possible because of the control over reproduction that technology has made possible. The aim of the radical feminists is total restructuring of society.

The abolition of capitalism and the institution of a socialist economy, while necessary, are not sufficient. Nor is it reforms in the status of women that are sought. "The end goal of feminist revolution must be..., not just the elimination of male privilege but of sex distinction itself : genital difference between human beings would no longer matter culturally[11] (Firestione 11). Thus all sex role stereotyping must be abolished.

Many radical feminists reject heterosexuality as a valid sexuality for free women. For them, men are the enemies. This radical feminism is frequently associated with lesbian sexuality. They advocate social, economical, political and psychological experimentation to usher in a new order of equal opportunity to everybody. Their strategies for liberation include the united struggle of women against men and male-dominated society. Lesbian feminism is now progressing in new directions, with the emphasis shifting to the imaginative identification of all women. This new shift is based on the theory that only a woman can understand another woman perfectly. This view transcends the issue of civil rights and sexual preferences. Lesbian feminism has now become a politics of asking women's questions demanding a world in which integrity of all women shall be honoured and validated in every aspect of culture.

Closely related to radical feminism is a philosophical branch of feminism which celebrates the intellect and temperament inherent in woman's nature as essentially different from a man's nature. They concern themselves mainly with a hidden female power that has great social relevance. They believe that when compared to men, women have greater concern and respect for human life. According to their notions women are the civilizers of this world. As it stresses an essential difference between the nature and purpose of men and women, this has been the most popular form of feminism among men.

The liberal feminists or Women's Rights Feminists believe that the inferior position of women is due to cultural and psychological factors. Although John Stuart Mill is considered the first liberal thinker championing the cause of woman, it was Mary Wollstonecraft, who in her book *Vindication of the Rights of Women* (1792) made many points which were later taken up by Mill. In this work, she attacks the educational restrictions and 'mistaken notions of female excellence' that keep women in a state of ignorance and slavish dependence. However, it is Mill's classic work, *The Subjection of Women* (1869) which became the Bible of the feminists in the latter part of the nineteenth century. It provided the movement with a philosophic rationale of cosmic proportions and, more than a century after its publication, stands unchallenged as the most distinguished intellectual monument the cause has yet produced. According to Mill, the subjection of women was the product of age-long custom and was not the proof of any inherent inferiority in them. 'All women', he writes:

> are brought up from the very earliest years in the belief that their ideal of character is the very opposite to that of men; not self will, and government by self-control, but submission, and yielding to the control of others. All the moralities tell them that it is the duty of women, and all the current sentimentalities that it is their nature, to live for others; to make complete abnegation of themselves, and to have no life but in their affections[12]. (V).

Like other liberals, Mill believed that equality between the two sexes can be brought about by moral reforms, education and legal measures. Among contemporaries, the views of Betty Freudian come nearest to this attitude. Moderate feminists have been relatively optimistic about working with men. Nevertheless, they believe that women must depend primarily on themselves."..... it would be as much of a mistake to expect men to hand this to women as to consider all men as the enemy, all men as oppressors"[13] (Freudian 36). Like "any other oppressed group," women must lead the fight for their own liberation.

While moderates are increasingly using the term "revolution" they do not mean it literally. A non-sexist society can be attained by working through the present system. Many may hope that an accumulation of reforms will transform society, but radical restructuring, such as that envisioned by the socialist or radical feminists, is not considered necessary.

In the third world countries, feminism has a very different set of concerns. With the history of colonization behind them, which had considerably mutilated their economy, the feminists from these countries engaged themselves in the task of liberating their women from oppressive cultural and religious conventions like purdah, sati, etc. The lack of proper education and the paralyzing influence of superstition are powerful antagonistic forces they confront. Although most of the third world countries differ politically, socially and economically from one another, there is often a similarity in their ideologies which result from a common colonial experience and which defines female labour as property of men. Survival in the third world invariably depends on the work that women do. Yet their labour has been undervalued and ignored. Whether waged or unwaged, female employment is subsumed by the family and controlled by ideologies that attach low status to women and their work.

As feminism is primarily a revolution in social consciousness, it affected literature and literary criticism from its earliest days. Feminist criticism has now become a fully established branch of literary studies. One section of feminist critics attempt re-readings of literature written by women to discover hidden expressions of feminist protest. As an interesting example of such an endeavour, we can point out the work of Susan Gubar and Gilbert Sandra who discover 'the mad woman in the Attic' *in Jane Eyre* as the concealed feminist protest in Bronte. Another section of feminist critics engaged themselves in the task of unearthing forgotten, unknown and unappreciated texts of literary importance. Recent research in this field has brought to limelight several significant female writers like Rokeya Hossein, whose works were for long ignored or considered insignificant. These critics take up re-reading of male texts, too, mostly to unearth the positive or negative attitudes to feminism that these works conceal. Kate Millet's reading of Henry Miller and Normal Mailer, which reveals their essential sexist view, is a pioneering work of this genre.

Another significant attempt in this field has been to discover a female tradition in literature. One of the pioneering studies in this field, that of Elain Showalter, is of particular relevance to this study. In her *A Literature of Their Own* (1977) she studies the works of the famous and not so famous British women writers and discovers a female tradition and subculture in English literature which has so far been overlooked by male critics.

According to Showalter, the development of this female tradition is similar to the development of any other literary subculture. She substantiates her argument with the new-found awareness that "female imagination" is not a Freudian abstraction but the product of a delicate network of influences operating in history. Showalter obviously draws on Fanon's study of colonial and racial subcultures which suggests that all literary subcultures — Black, colonial, etc. — go through three major phases. The first one is of imitation, in which artists and intellectuals in the subculture blindly imitate the norms of the dominant tradition, internalizing its standards of art and its views on society and in so doing, legitimize their claim to human equality. In the female tradition, Showalter names this stage 'the feminine phase'. The leading female writers of this phase portrayed their heroines as 'ideal' women -- as the angel in the house, surviving on sacrifice, endurance and passive subservience.

The second phase of literary subculture is generally one of protest against the dominating standards and values. Such protest is manifested mainly through the advocacy of minority rights and values including demands for autonomy. Showalter calls this stage of the female literary tradition the 'feminist' phase. This stage coincides with the upsurge of the first wave of feminist movements and most of the works that Showalter includes in this phase openly demand better status and more freedom for women.

The third and the most important phase is one of a search for, what Showalter calls, a genuine identity. It is in this stage that the quest for freedom is turned inward and aimed at the goal of self-discovery. But she makes it clear that these categories are not rigid and quite often they overlap. Sometimes, all the three may appear in a single writer. Often the third stage, the female phase of courageous self-exploration, carries with it the double legacy of feminine self-hatred and feminist withdrawal. It marks the development of a separatist, woman-centred literature of inner space. It is psychologically rather than socially focussed and Showalter observes that the novels of this phase exhibit the recurrence of the symbol of an enclosed or secret room.

A discussion of feminism will remain inconclusive without considering what may be termed as the 'paradox of feminism'. The crusaders of the feminist movement believed that with the emergence of the fully emancipated woman who is intellectually man's equal, who is economically independent, and who has discarded all her shackles, woman will attain her real status in society, a status based on security, dignity and freedom. This was their cherished hope but the facts, as they are today, belie such a hope.

As the society marches onward the gender factor exerts a greater pull to the disadvantage of women. The role of the gender factor in poverty has emerged in several recent studies on poverty. Instead of economic parity with men, women are being pushed below the poverty line. In the Indian scene a study describes this situation as 'poverty within poverty.' This is not the case only with developing countries. Even in the U. S. this phenomenon is becoming more and more obvious. One such study has termed the phenomenon in the U. S. as the 'feminization of poverty'[14] (Thurow 26).

Even achievement of economic independence does not guarantee emancipation from male-dominance. Rather, the economically independent, educated, emancipated modern woman finds herself burdened with even greater shackles. Ajita Garg has termed it as 'woman doubly enslaved'[15] (24-27) — enslavement on the domestic front and enslavement on the employment front.

The girl-child, even in the educated families, continues to suffer due to gender discrimination while the educated housewife's lot is no better. In many cases she is treated as an instrument of augmenting her husband's income thereby justifying the remark in the *Communist Manifesto* that 'the bourgeois sees in his wife a mere instrument of production'. The increase in the number of bride burning and dowry deaths is a sad commentary on their lot.

Outside the family, woman is being reduced more and more to the level of a commodity. The obsession to exploit a woman's body for advertisement and sales promotion is taking away the last shreds of the dignity of her person. In the so-called civilized societies crimes against women are on the increase. So, in the modern society, women still do not enjoy security, dignity or freedom in the real sense.

Engels has put the situation in the right perspective when he observes :

. . . That woman was the slave of man at the commencement of society is one of the most absurd notions that have come down to us from the period of Enlightenment of the eighteenth century. Woman occupied not only a free but also a highly respected position among all savages and all barbarians. Peoples whose women have to work much harder than we would consider proper often have far more real respect for women than our Europeans have for theirs. The social status of the lady of civilization, surrounded by sham homage and estranged from all real work, is socially infinitely lower than that of the hard-working woman of barbarism[16] (Marx and Engels 481-82)

This predicament of the 'new woman' is an important concern of the women novelists that have been included in this study. For the purpose of this study, therefore, the ideal of the feminist movement as the modern emancipated woman is not necessarily the concept of the 'new woman' although she might share some of the traits of the emancipated woman, yet she is something more.

Therefore, it is essential to examine the question in what respects the 'new woman' is new.

(ii) CONCEPT OF THE 'NEW WOMAN'

The 'new woman' of our study is not the contemporary woman or even the modern woman. The concept of modernity keeps changing from time to time and from one social milieu to another. The roles of women as well as men undergo a change along with the change in the above-mentioned parameters. These parameters are the set of contingencies which determine the changing roles of the persons who are governed by these contingencies. In this sense every age will have its modern woman, who might not necessarily be the 'new woman'.

In the works selected for this study there are women characters who in every sense are modern yet they can't be viewed as representatives of the 'new woman'. The study points out such characters who are modern but not 'new'. Side by side there are characters who can't be called modern yet they belong to the category of the 'new woman'.

Also the 'new woman' of the present study is not a projection of the modern feminist movement into literary characters. However, the feminist theories, which although originated in the West, are valid for all societies. These are the socialist theories, especially those of Marx and Engels. Even the most emancipated and modern characters of the study do not give evidence of the consciousness of the feminist movement. But the authors under study are all not only aware of the feminist movement but all of them to some extent, and some of them entirely, are the embodiments of the emancipated woman of the feminist movement. Therefore, if the characters sometimes display an awareness of the feminist movement, it may be a case of the author projecting herself into them.

A woman is 'new' if her basic concerns are deeper than merely seeking equality with men, asserting her own personality and insisting upon her own rights as a woman. Seen from this angle, even a rebel or a revolutionary woman cannot be called a 'new woman' on this account alone. The woman is 'new ' when she analyses and reflects upon her position essentially as a woman in the scheme of things which includes the social, moral and spiritual fields.

However, it is not only the 'new woman' who reflects along these lines. Every woman, at some time or other, does the same but such reflections are conditioned by the thought-patterns handed down to her by moral, intellectual and social order which has been formed by man. The 'new woman' not only reflects on her position as a woman in the scheme of things but at the same time she does not use the thought-patterns given to her by this male-made order. She attempts to evolve her own thinking process, her own intellectual pattern in such a reflection. This she generally does through the use of metaphors. The characters of Kamala Markandaya and Anita Desai use such metaphors in reflecting on the scheme of things. The metaphors reveal the moral and spiritual urge of the 'new woman'. These metaphors deal with the themes of suffering, dominance, urge for companionship, etc. It is through these that the moral and spiritual needs of the 'new woman' are projected.

These women also explore the entire domain of their family life, their social and inter-personal relationships, their roles as daughters, sisters, wives and mothers in a new frame of reference which they have evolved for themselves. They also evolve their own 'moral code' in the light of which they evaluate the social norms set by the society. This, however, might not always be conscious. Therefore, the entire gamut of the social norms of man-made social order which are the bases of evaluating the various roles imposed upon woman are also covered. But this evaluation in the 'new woman' is secondary to the examination of her moral and spiritual needs. The analyses of the novels of Kamala Markandaya and Anita Desai seek to explore this aspect.

However, the modern woman having remained suppressed for thousands of years might be tempted to level her score with man in the present social order and so she might even demonstrate that she can not only have her way in all matters but she can also beat man at his own game of gender dominance, which may be characterised as the 'Moll Flanders syndrome'.

But at the very roots this has only a negative significance. It is a sort of reaction which ignores the moral and spiritual quest the study seeks to investigate as the important trait of the 'new woman'. However, the temptation to label such characters as the 'new woman' is there. This study considers such characters as "aberrations", which do not bring out the essential positive traits of the 'new woman'. But even in such modern women there is evidence of the awareness of moral and spiritual needs, though they might be hidden beneath the glamour of the emancipated modern woman. So in some respects, even these women can be considered as representatives of the 'new woman' because a deeper analysis of these characters reveals the existence of these needs at the core while the life of glamour and modernity is only at the periphery of their psyche.

In the literature of the modern age the first example of the 'new woman' is Nora of Ibsen's play, *A Doll's House*. But even Nora is not a 'new woman' until the last part of the play. Before that she is a conventional housewife accepting the moral code for nineteenth century women. She also accepts her role which the man-made social system has set for her. She becomes a 'new woman' when she tells her husband, Helmer "Let us sit down and discuss"[17] (Ibsen 85). This is the moment when she has suddenly developed a new insight into the man-made social order and the position of a woman in it. She suddenly sees her role as a woman, a wife, a mother in a new perspective which is condensed in a single phrase 'a dolls' house' and she leaves this *'doll's house'* to discover herself. Yet this insight only covers the domain of the social order while the 'new women' of our study go beyond the consideration of the social order and their position in it.

It is not in modern literature only that we come across a woman analysing her role as a woman and reflecting on her position in the light of such an analysis. Homer's *Iliad* is perhaps the first example in Western literature where we meet such a situation. And it is Helen of Troy who perceives her position in this light. Whenever she refers to herself in *The Iliad*, she never does so without using such expressions as 'my abhorred and miserable self' (Book III), 'my unhappy self' (Book XIV). Although she is reflecting on her own lot, yet it is significant that the woman, who to male eyes symbolised nothing but attraction and physical charm, sees hereself in a totally different light. Even the 'elders of Troy', who were too old to fight, are struck by her beauty (Book III). Faustus is enraptured at the vision of her face :

> Was this the face that launched a thousand ships, And burnt the topless towers of Ilium?
>
> O Helen! make me immortal with a kiss [18] (*Faustus* V.1.99-101).

This shows how man is incapable of fathoming a woman's psyche, much less of appreciating it.

The Iliad gives further insight into women be-wailing their own lot while appearing to weep for someone else. The Greeks, during the course of their ten-year siege of Troy, had sacked many other towns in the neighbourhood and had brought their women to their camp and divided them up among themselves. When the Greek hero, Patroclus is slain (Book XIX) these 'bonds women' lament over his dead body 'making as though their tears were for Patroclus, but in truth each was weeping for her own sorrows'[19] *(Iliad 273)*. This shows how in the male-dominated society a woman has to evolve the indirect technique of expressing her sorrow through projecting it as the grief for some other person. Thus, women are forced to evolve their own pattern of exteriorizing their feelings.

Homer is the father of epic and Aristotle has called him the father of tragedy and also of comedy. It may also be added that he is the first male to develop an insight into women's psyche which the women novelists of our study, too, attempt to provide.

It would be worthwhile exploring how the aforesaid traits of the 'new woman' feature in each of the four authors under study. The women characters of Kamala Markandaya's novels, though not conscious, though not fully aware, yet are concerned with the fundamental question — the lot of women. This they analyse through the metaphor of dominance or through the metaphor of suffering. In this sense, it gives evidence of a new kind of thinking which finds full flowering in later writers. Also, when subjected to stresses and strains, both internal and external, the women characters evolve a set of responses to protect their psyche from being bruised, thus giving credence to the fact that every woman need evolve her own defense mechanism in this world of male dominance.

In the novels of Anita Desai taken up for the study, nearly all women figure in the first person narrative, yet they don't assume the form of a narrative. The woman who tells the story is not concerned about incidents or facts as happens in a narrative but is more concerned about her reaction — moral, spiritual and emotional. This going deeper into her own personality or exploring her own self is the trait of the 'new woman'. The attempt at self-realization may or may not lead to self-fulfilment, yet it does not invalidate her quest. Like the traditional woman, the 'new woman', too, tolerates, makes adjustments for the family and the husband, understands him and even forgives him but nowhere do we find her changing or moulding her basic personality. In this sense, the 'new woman' of Anita Desai is very much like her male counterpart who may be tolerating, may be indifferent, may even revolt but never changing his basic personality for the sake of his wife or the family. Basically, the woman protagonists of Desai's fiction aim at spiritual fulfilment which may be analysed through various metaphors such as that of barrenness, moon, violence, etc. Also, her heroines enter the domain of speculative philosophy thereby exploding the myth that it is only the preserve of the male. An insight into the consciousness of Desai's women characters reveals that they seem to be toying with the idea as to whether it is possible to reconstruct the social order based on the psyche of woman. In this regard, her novels are in themselves a metaphor of deconstruction, for in deconstruction reconstruction is inherent.

Lastly, the women characters of Namita Gokhale and Shobha De can in all likelihood pass for 'new women' since most of them are economically independent and socially emancipated. Judged in terms of one feminist school of thought, they deserve the epithet, for in every walk of life right from earning a living to most blatant issues of sexuality, they are on a level of parity with their male counterparts. However, when compared with the manner in which the women characters of Kamala Markandaya and Anita Desai are 'new', the women characters of Namita Gokhale and Shobha De appear to be an 'aberration'.

The woman protagonists of these two novelists consider men as the source of enjoyment. But this metaphor i.e. the opposite sex as the source of enjoyment, is essentially a metaphor which is a part of male dominance. Hence, by borrowing a metaphor from the male world and treating men's value-systems as theirs, they are actually doing nothing 'new'. This is reflected in their not feeling guilty or remorse after having an illicit relationship outside marriage; they may even boast about it or just forget about it or might even publicize it and parade their sexuality and become ready again to begin their life anew — so far all these were part of male prerogatives, but these women have challenged the value-systems of male dominance and adopted them as theirs. This they consider as self-fulfilling or a source of self-fulfilment. But even in these novelists, the women characters do throw a glimpse here and there that this kind of life cannot become a source of spiritual fulfilment or even provide lasting peace or comfort. Even they realise that this does not and to the enrichment of their personality. So, they are not the kind of women we are looking for.

If it were not so, after Anita Desai, we should have found women, who would attain spiritual realization but the study of Namita Gokhale and Shobha De, who appear later than Anita Desai on the fiction scene in the chronological order, does not proceed in that direction. Hence, we are justified in calling their women characters an 'aberration' so far as the concept of the 'new woman' is concerned.

NOTES

1. Alix Kate Shulman, "Dancing in the Revolution : Emma Goldman's Feminism," *Socialist Review* Mar. -Apr. 1982 : 32-33.

2. Kate Millet, *Sexual Politics* (London : Virgo, 1972) 60.

3. Marx and Engels, "The Origin of Family, Private Property and State," *Selected Works* (Moscow : Progress Publishers, 1982) 495.

4. Marx and Engels 50.

5. Juliet Mitchell, "Women -- The Longest Revolution", *From Feminism to Liberation* (Schekman : Cambridge Mass, 1971) 123.

6. Betty and Theodore Roszak, " 'Red Stockings' Manifesto", *Masculine/ Feminine* (New York : Harper and Row, 1969).

7. Shulamith Firestone, *The Dialectic of Sex* (New York : Bantam, 1970) 8.

8. Firestone 8.

9. Firestone 8.

10. Firestone 9.

11. Firestone 11.

12. Wendell R. Carr, Introduction, *The Subjection of Women,* by John Stuart Mill (Cambridge : M.I.T. Press, 1970) 36.

13. Betty Freudian, "Our Renolution is Unique", *Voice of the New Ferminism* ed. Mary Lou Thomson (Boston : Beacon, 1970) 36.

14. Lester C. Thurow, "A Surge in Inequality", *Scientific American* May 1987, 256.5 : 26.

15. Ajita Garg, "Women Doubly Enslaved", *Social Welfare* (M) Aug. 1988 : 24-27.

16. Marx and Engels, 481-82.
17. Henrik Ibsen, *A Doll's House,* trans. Archer et al., ed. Francis Bull (London : Centenary, 1963), Act iii, 85.
18. Christopher Marlowe, *Doctor Faustus,* ed. Kitty Datta (Delhi : O.U.P., 1980), Act V, Sc.i, lines 99-101, 146.
19. Homer, *The Iliad of Homer,* trans. Samuel Butler, ed. Louise Ropes Loomis (New York : Classic Club, 1942), 273.

3

ANTICIPATING THE 'NEW WOMAN'

Any study of Kamala Markandaya would remain incomplete without the 'woman subject', for in her novels it is the woman who occupies the central place. Most of her works have women narrators or, like Jane Austen's novels, the story is narrated through feminine consciousness. H. M. Williams aptly observes that Markandaya "has a particular interest in analysing women characters and suggesting the unusual poignancy of their fate"[1] (28). She confines herself to the narrow range of experience within the four walls of the domestic set-up and "evinces a keen interest in the relationship of the individual and society, in the way this relationship is mediated through the family, in the possibilities and mechanisms of change in the individual and thus in society at large"[2] (Geetha 126).

An analysis of her novels reveals that she is 'feminine' in her perspective, in the sense in which Sharon Spencer defines the word. According to Spencer, "the adjective 'feminine' when applied to literature nowadays customarily indicates the author's pre occupation with intimate human relationships, concern with the emotional aspects of life and with the dynamics of the psychic realm of experiencce"[3] (157). This definition of the 'feminine' closely approximates with the experiences of the 'new woman' in the manner she has been suggested in the earlier chapter.

Kamala Markandaya's investigation and presentation of a feminine consciousness is mainly directed towards an objective account of woman's emotions against the background of the Indian woman's emerging awareness of her identity in a male-dominated social and moral order. Some of the circumstances reported in Markandaya's fiction give evidence of her intense awareness of her identity as a woman and her attention to feminine problems. This concern about the contemporary women's lives, women's concerns, is worth noting and that is what makes us apply the term 'feminism' in its broadest sense to her works. She is not a radical feminist and her novels are not an outright condemnation of a repressive male-dominated society calling for reconstruction of male-female roles. Nor are they naturalistic accounts of the victimisation of women. "Kamala Markandaya's attitude to feminism is established as personal, analytic and exploratory rather than public, political or polemical"[4] (Geetha 127).

She does not create a world. She presents the world as it is, posing serious questions about contemporary attitudes to men, women and marriage. She investigates the actual social and emotional bonds that shackle women. Indian woman in her novels defines herself by a set of relationships and modes of conduct within a created society. She confronts a tradition-oriented society and learns to live under the twin whips of heritage and modernity. "Despite the changes in norms, the impact of western culture, and alien mores, economic and social progress, she is essentially Indian in sensibility"[5] (Geetha 127) and yet she "picks up enough courage to raise her head and ask a few awkward but pertinent questions, and the responses would determine the shift towards new development strategies in the Indian social polity"[6] (Krishnaswamy 8). In her novels, Kamala Markandaya presents the liberalising aspect of this change in the attitude of women. The present study precisely addresses itself to this change in woman's attitude in so far as her awareness of her own position in a male-dominated society in particular and of her position in the scheme of things in general is concerned. This awareness is not expressed as a conscious affirmation of her realization of the woman's position. This awareness is not even verbalised in this form in her own mind. We may, therefore, say that she is anticipating the 'new woman'.

As a searching analyst of women's roles, Kamala Markandaya underlines the traditional attitude to women in her novels. In *Some Inner Fury* the novelist refers to the silent barriers against women :

> There is a tradition not only in India, that women should not be worried, that the best way to ensure this is to keep them as far as possible in ignorance... Certain domains belong to men alone, and Indian women learn early not to encroach[7]. (Markandaya 117)

Through this Kamala Markandaya seems to be suggesting that the women would no longer remain 'in ignorance', 'certain domains' no longer 'belong to men alone' and women, too, are beginning to 'learn' 'to encroach'. The 'new woman' in her novels gives an insight into this kind of awareness, although she herself is unaware of it.

In the tradition set by women novelists like Jane Austen, Kamala Markandaya also believes that the truth of human relations can be best expressed in terms of social institutions such as marriage and family. The importance of domestic life and the integrity of the family form an important part of her fiction. Marriage for Kamala Markandaya seems to be a profound symbol of community and marriage in her fiction has been "the woman's adventure, the object of her quest, her journey's end"[8] (Heiburn 309). The early novels, *Nectar in a Sieve* and *A Handful of Rice* seem to present the wife in the traditional role. But underlying this suffering, sacrificial role is the 'new woman', who wishes to suggest that a woman is more than a mother, wife or housekeeper. Over and above her children, her husband or the house she has a soul with an emotional and a spiritual urge in it. In almost all her novels, the author sets forth an inspiring goal — "autonomy for the self, nurturance for the family and fellow feeling for the community of men and women"[9] (Krishnaswamy 163). This autonomy for the self need not always make the woman economically independent and socially emancipated but it certainly gives a peep into "autonomy" of attitudes pertaining to certain vital moral, social and spiritual aspects of life. Such thinking is independent of "social conditioning" to which a woman is subjected by a male-oriented social order. It is in this sense that her women characters are "new". What Diana Trilling writes about the novels of Murdoch can be equally well applied to the novels of Kamala Markandaya :

> It is not the quest for female selfhood but implicitly the need we all have for a new way of being, a new social and moral consciousness. She is not a sexual liberationist, she is a non-dogmatic, non-polemical social revolutionary for whom the affectless pan-sexuality of her characters is the symbol[10] (510).

This 'new way of being' of which Diana Trilling talks, the women in Kamala Markandaya's novels seem to 'achieve' by showing a consciousness both at the spiritual as well as at the mundane levels. At the spiritual level the 'new woman' in her novels reflects on such important aspects as the lot of woman, her position in a male-dominated society, her need for companionship based on sympathy, understanding and love, the urge for spiritual fulfilment, etc. On the social, domestic and emotional fronts, too, evidence of "new" thinking can be noticed. But quite often her ideas on these subjects, both spiritual and mundane, are overlapping. Therefore, any discussion on the 'new woman' in Kamala Markandaya's novels cannot be done on well-demarcated aspectual lines. All the same, what is possible is the presentation of an overall view of her consciousness — moral, social, spiritual — which can put her in the category of the 'new woman'. The novels selected for an in-depth study, *Nectar in a Sieve, Two Virgins* and *A Handful of Rice* seem to be precisely doing this job.

In *Nectar in a Sieve* [11] we have the stresses produced by the coming up of the tannery on the rural society and so on one level the novel can be studied as dwelling upon the theme of urbanization of Indian villages and its disastrous impact on human life in India. It also takes on the dimension of neo-colonization after independence which meant a total suspension of Gandhian values envisioned before 1947. This is one direction along which the development in the novel takes place and the movement of the incidents to a large extent takes place along these lines. And as this phenomenon—a new element such as the tannery, the urbanization of the villages, the collapse of traditional values—was witnessed all over the country, the contemporary literature and also the literature of other Indian languages reflected it and Indo-English literature was no exception.

But there is another and a deeper side involving the psyche of the woman, which is independent of this phenomenon but which is more fundamental and which is relevant even in the present context of the position of woman. And it is with this aspect that the novel's main concern seems to lie. The only difference is that the woman here is not acutely aware of her lot or position.

Nectar in a Sieve is essentially a tale of village life as comprehended through a female sensibility. Rukmani is the first peasant woman Markandaya presents. Her tale could be any village woman's tale in India of the fifties. But what Markandaya does is that she invests Rukmani with a sharper sensitivity which enables her to understand her own position and also that of her fellow-sufferers of the same sex in this male-made social set-up. Right in the beginning, we find Rukmani confronted with a social problem when she gives birth to her first child who happens to be a daughter. In her ignorance, at first she gives vent to her disappointment by saying, "What woman wants a girl for her first born?" (*NS* 14). Even her neighbour Kali sympathises with her and consoles her, "Never mind. There will be many later on. You have plenty of time" (*NS* 14). But this disappointment is not at the core of her personality. Later, when she is reflecting retrospectively on this event of her life, she gives evidence of her actual thinking on the subject :

> ... I am ashamed that I ever had such thoughts : my only excuse is that thoughts come of their own accord, although afterwards we can chase them away (*NS* 14).

So whatever 'disappointment' or anguish she experienced as a young lady for not providing her husband with a male heir as their first-born, she considerably modifies her thinking as a mature person. In this way she indirectly reflects on the predicament faced by every woman, rural or urban, namely that of providing a male-heir to the family. In her reflection, thus, she seems to be much ahead of her times.

If society does not look favourably at a woman who is unable to provide a male-heir, it is even harsher on those who are barren. Rukmani can very well identify herself with the lot of such a woman, for in her early life she had experienced this kind of a gloomy situation. After the birth of her first daughter Ira, she realised that she wouldn't be able to conceive any more. But this did not dampen her spirits, and she approached Kenny, the Scottish doctor for medical aid and got cured. Now a similar lot befalls her own daughter, Ira who is sent back from her in-laws' house, for 'she is a barren woman'. The conversation that takes place between the mother and the daughter after the latter's husband deserts her is poignant in as much as it puts the issue of barrenness in perspective from the point of view of Rukmani. Ira asks her mother to let her alone :

> "Leave me alone, Mother. I have seen this coming for a long time. The reality is much easier to bear than the imagining. At least now there is no more fear no more necessity for lies and concealment."

> "There should never have been," I said. "Are we not your parents? Did you think we would blame you for what is not your fault?"
> "There are others," she replied. "Neighbours, women ... and I a failure, a woman who cannot even bear a child" (*NS* 50).

As if in complete identification with the suffering of all those women who 'cannot even bear a child' and are blamed for no fault of theirs, she comments : "All this I had gone through - the torment, the anxiety. Now the whole dreadful story was repeating itself, and it was my daughter this time" (*NS* 50).

The above-mentioned piece of conversation acquires significance for one more reason. In addition to its comment on a woman's lot and her suffering, it also reveals one more facet of a woman's personality. Since she has to face more problems in life than her male counterpart, she evolves her own set of responses or defense-mechanisms to meet these situations. Ira's observation that, "... The reality is much easier to bear than the imaginings. At least now there is no more fear, no more necessity for lies and concealment" — is nothing but part of her defense-mechanism to put up with the kind of situation she finds herself in. Another character in the novel who resorts to defense-mechanism is the vegetable seller, Old Granny. She is the one who had arranged the match for Ira and hence she is more upset about the outcome of her marriage than anyone else. As if owning some kind of implicit moral responsibility for this failure, she feels guilty. But Rukmani tells her that it is neither her fault, nor her daughter's or her husband's, it is fate. But she is more worried about the girl's future. To this the old lady replies, "Why fear?" "Am I not alone and do I not manage?" (*NS* 62). She further adds that, "It is not unbearable." "One gets used to it" (NS 62). Thus, Old Granny's views not only suggest that she is able to put up with her single status bravely but that such a situation, that is, living alone as a female all one's life, is not at all a terrifying experience as it is generally imagined to be and that it is quite bearable and one easily gets used to it. Here it is worth noting that even such an illiterate woman as the Old Granny has her own views on the status of a single woman leading an independent life. The 'new' element in this awareness further springs from the fact that the views come from the mouth of a person who belongs to a tradition-oriented, taboo-ridden society.

That a woman needs something more than her material comforts is driven home to us through Rukmani's description of rich Muslim women who were the wives of the officials of the tannery. Describing them she says :

> ... living midway between the town and open country in brick cottages with whitewashed walls and red-tiled roofs -- the women

- well, they were a queer lot, and their way of life was quite different from ours. What they did in the houses I do not know, for they employed servants to do the work; but they stayed mostly indoors or if they went out at all they went *veiled in bourkas*. It was their religion, I was told : they would not appear before any man but told: they would not appear before any man but their husband. Sometimes, when I caught sight of a figure in voluminous draperies swishing through the streets under a blazing sun, or of a face peering through the window of a shutter, *I felt* desperately sorry for them, deprived of the ordinary pleasures of knowing warm sun and cool breeze upon their flesh, of walking out light and free, or of mixing with men and working beside them. (*NS* 48)

Thus it is the woman in Rukmani alone that can understand the plight of such women - what they suffer and what they miss in life. It is a reaction very different from men reflecting on a similar situation. But in the novel itself we have other women like Kali who cannot rise above the earthly, material concerns. From her point of view :

"They (these Muslim women) have their compensations, ... it is any easy life, with no worry for the next meal and plenty always at hand. I would gladly wear bourka and walk veiled for the rest of my life if I, too, could be sure of such things" (*NS* 48).

Rukmani, used as she is 'to open fields and the sky and the unfettered sight of the sun', thinks in much more basic terms :

"Who could endure such a filtering of sun light and fresh air as they do?" (*NS* 48). To her, 'warm sun and cool breeze' symbolize freedom to which every human being feels entitled. Depriving an individual of these basic 'necessities' amounts to denying him the freshness of life and all that it stands for -- it is a great impediment in the realization of an individual's spiritual needs.

Even on the role of physical relationship in marital life Rukmani's thoughts are directed towards emotional and spiritual fulfilment. In a traditional society a women talking about her experience in the act of love is something which is rare even today. But Rukmani does so giving full evidence of her mature thinking on this vital aspect of life. In her kind of society, sex becomes something of a torture to a woman who is past middle-age but even at this juncture for her it is a fulfilling experience :

In the straining darkness I felt his body moving with desire, his hands on me were trembling, and I felt my senses opening like flower to his urgency. I closed my eyes and waited, waited in the darkness while my being filled with a wild, ecstatic fluttering, waited for him to come (*NS* 57)

Hence, for her, sex does not remain a source of mere physical gratification. It is neither mechanical nor a ritual to be performed at the behest of her husband's demands — it is something higher. At this stage it becomes a sort of fulfilment which is singular and unique to her personality. Thus, Rukmani's views on sex are akin to those of even an ultra modern woman. Modern or traditional, all women look for sex as a source of spiritual and emotional fulfilment. It is a part of the core element of every woman's personality.

The relationship between Rukmani and the Scottish doctor Kennington (referred to as Kenny in the novel) needs a detailed discussion in so far as it gives insight into the desire of every individual — male or female — to call something of one's own, something which one cherishes exclusively all by oneself. Rukmani's relationship with Kenny is not viewed by her as part of 'East-West relationship', as has been suggested by H. S. Mahle[12] (99-110). Actually she is not even aware of it. She does not have the slightest realisation the she is doing something 'new' — it is only that she does not wish to share this part of her relationship with anyone. It is true that she goes to Kenny for treatment of infertility and subsequently bears five sons to her husband, Nathan. But her visits do not in any way weigh on her conscience. She does not consider them immoral by any standards, although in the context of her village background any relationship with any other man, much less a foreigner, was against the accepted standards of normal conduct.

The best part is that Rukmani does not experience an inner conflict even while she does not divulge the fact of her relationship with Kenny to her husband. When Kenny comes on a visit she introduces him to her husband, Nathan in a casual way without any feeling of guilt, "You have heard me tell of Kenny often enough. This is he, friend to my father's house" (*NS* 33). Later also when Kenny is on the verge of disclosing that Rukmani had been to him for treatment, the latter feels no sense of 'betrayal' on her part.

Rukmani's relationship with Kenny is based on friendship, intimacy and understanding. Rukmani, ever since her mother was treated by Dr. Kenny, had felt drawn towards him. "He was tall and gaunt with a pale skin and sunken eyes the colour of a kingfisher's wing, neither blue nor green" (*NS* 19). He was the man in whom Rukmani' mother had faith. "Between her and this man, young though he was, lay mutual understanding and respect, one for the other, (*NS* 19). He came to her father's house often, sometimes even when he was not summoned. He told her no lies, and she trusted him. Since then, for sometime there developed a relationship of faith and fear between Rukmani and Kenny. Soon the fear was dispelled. Rukmani's going to Kenny for treatment and begetting a child brought a complete transformation in her life. She started taking Kenny as her patron and benefactor. She said, "My lord, my benefactor, many a time I have longed to see you, now at last you come" (*NS* 31). She bent down to his feet, stood as he was, in leather shoes. When Kenny said that he was not her benefactor, nor a lord, she replied, "You are my benefactor. Have I not five sons to prove it?" (*NS* 31).

Rukmani stood under great obligation to Kenny. Again and again she told him, " You have done so much for me and mine". "Your presence means a lot to us" (*NS* 107). She was grateful to Kenny for bringing food and milk for her children and husband. Kenny loved children. She said, "Mine were always eager to see him, making great fun of him when he came, and he for his part would suffer them patiently, often bringing with him half a coconut or 'laddus' made of nuts and rolled into balls with jaggery, which the children loved" (*NS* 33).

Kenny made the barren Ira fertile, got jobs for Rukmani's sons and took one of them as his own assistant. In fact he was a fairy God father to the family of Nathan and Rukmani. She had garlands for him as so many had and held a "lemon" for him to save him from "evil tongues" and "evil eyes". And kenny, too, "felt for her".

Personally Kenny had friendly feelings for Rukmani and her family and it was reciprocated by Rukmani's "feeling; very deep, very tender for this man" (*NS* 107). The two were friends, Rukmani holding him in respect. Thus it can be seen that "the encounter between them is not just a simple one of straight-forward, predetermined categories held in clear-cut opposition to one another, but there is a human bond that cuts across all barriers of race and religion, of sex and skin, of nationality and culture"[13] (Goyal 108).

As far as Rukmani is concerned, questions such as those of morality or propriety of the relationship between her and Kenny do not even occur to her. To her the relationship is a natural one of companionship. She can share her thoughts and problems with Kenny on a mutual basis. There is no self-consciousness, much less any kind of embarrassment in this relationship. She is not conscious of him as a white man, or even as a man. He is only a friend with whom she can discuss her problems and share her thoughts in a manner she cannot do even with her husband; she does not share her feelings for Kenny with her husband. Yet we cannot say that she is concealing something from him. In fact, it does not even occur to her that there is anything to conceal. She introduces Kenny to her family in a quite natural way without any feeling of embarrassment. The entire domain of this relationship is beyond the moral and social code of the traditional woman. Her not sharing it with anyone might suggest that there is something in her mind which she wants to keep as her own and only her own. Not sharing it with anyone else is only an urge to assert her individuality as a person and as a woman. Hence, it is not concealment or keeping a secret. Rediscovering, redefining and asserting her identity as a person is a significant trait of the 'new woman'. The techniques for its realisation might vary from mere awareness to conscious affirmation. Although Rukmani does not verbalize her feelings in these terms yet the tremors are audible, however faintly, which in the later novelists will become a powerful declaration. Hence, we can say Rukmani is anticipating the 'new woman'.

If Rukmani's consciousness, both aware as well as unaware, suggests that she is anticipating the 'new woman' socially, emotionally and spiritually, it is Ira who represents the modern progressive woman in the novel. Young women like her trust their own judgement and stand on their feet. In times of acute famine, necessity drives Ira to trade her flesh. For her, "preservation of life is a matter of greater sanctity than the observance of a false morality"[14] (Goyal 106). Her father, Nathan rages with fury when he learns of it and forbids Ira to go out for her nightly rounds. But Ira says stubbornly : "Tonight and tomorrow and every night, so long as there is need. I will not hunger any more" (*NS* 99). Nathan strongly objects to her becoming a 'harlot', 'a common strumpet', but Ira stands defiantly and says : "These are but words ... There are other, kinder ones which for decency's sake ..."(*NS* 99). Words can be real tyrants, and what Ira stresses here is that "the aesthetics of semantics should be guided and determined by the ethics of survival"[15] (Goyal 106).

Thus Ira defies everybody and sticks to her way of life. She also shows the will power and mental strength to bring forth the Albino child she conceives outside her wedlock. "She is simply being herself in choosing her own life... That is a move of the Indian woman towards liberation"[16] (Geetha 133).

Of all her novels Kamala Markandaya's *Two Virgins*[17] expresses her concern with women's situation in modern India most sharply. The novel is written from the point of view of Saroja, although Markandaya focuses more sharply on Lalitha's fate. *Two Virgins* is a story about two sisters, Lalitha and Saroja, who grow from childhood to womanhood through adolescence. During this journey, their immediate environment, viz., members of their family, the village inhabitants, their schools, and far away influences such as those of the city and what it stands for, shape and reshape their ideas regarding different aspects of a woman's life. In the process each of the two sisters reaches a different conclusion about life. In addition to these two sisters, we have some minor yet important women characters whose points of view help the two main characters understand certain complex issues of life in perspective.

Lalitha, the older of the two, is a student of the village public-school. Being 'pretty and pert', she is aware of her beauty and its hold over people around her. Her beauty earns her a lot of favours at home which are denied to her plain-looking younger sister, Saroja. So, when Lalitha's school teacher, Miss Mendoza tells her parents that their 'exceptional daughter' deserves a career which is 'away from the dreary and the conventional', Lalitha at once starts imagining herself 'a golden eagle soaring over the plains'. For her, the opportunity comes with the arrival of Mr. Gupta, the film magnate on the village scene. Mr. Gupta instils in her the idea of a film career and Lalitha, in pursuit of stardom, goes to the city where she is spoilt by this film director. Gupta betrays her after she becomes pregnant.

What happens in the village a little before this tragic fate befalls Lalitha in the city is worth recalling. When Mr. Gupta visits their house, Lalitha draws a colam pattern'[18] to welcome him. The pattern of a dove on a trellis in the garden reflects her own ambitious imaginings about her rosy future. But Gupta unconsciously reflects the hard fate she is going to suffer at his hands. "When Mr. Gupta shuffled his feet the dove got blurred" (*TV* 107). One single unintentional step by Gupta destroys the beautiful pattern and he hardly notices what he has done. Similarly, a single move from Gupta destroys the whole life of Lalitha.

The beautiful little image foreshadows (anticipates) the future course of action. Lalitha goes with Gupta with the ambitious aim of becoming an actress. There she loses her head and becomes a victim of sex. Fearing the reproaches of society, she could not face going back to the village. Even though her parents try to get the abortion done in secret, the whole course of her life changes. She chooses her own society because "she had catapulted herself outside the orbit of her community" (*TV* 239). In the image of the 'colam', Lalitha repairs the damage done to the pattern of the dove and it turns out to be an eagle and this eagle represents the turn the stream of her life takes.

The plight of Lalitha in the society is foretold through the metaphor of suffering quite early in the novel. This is illustrated through the image of the monkey. The monkeys are attracted to their compound when the trees bear fruit. When scared away by stoning, a baby monkey gets hurt. It is abandoned by its mother and the rest of the tribe. The mother leaves it to die as "the tribe would never accept a cripple, not properly, that is, though it might manage to tolerate one" (*TV* 18). That is exactly the plight of Lalitha. With her illegal relationship with Gupta, she is crippled morally. She has no place in the society and she is left to suffer all alone.

Lalitha, thus, fits in the definition of the liberated heroine given by Diana Trilling in her article "The Liberated Heroine":

> She the liberated heroine is the fictional creation whose first concern is the exploration and realisation of female selfhood; this investigation of self undertakes to be independent of the traditional dictates of society as these pertain to female behaviour and the relation of sexes [19] ... (501)

But Lalitha comes to realize that her liberation was a myth. She succumbs to the temptations of sex because she is too conscious of the freedom conferred by the new social dispensation. Through Lalitha, Kamala Markandaya seems to hint that on the one hand, women have quite the same right as men have to be messy, trivial and self-deceiving and on the other hand, that "messiness, triviliality and false rhetoric of the emotions dehumanise women no less than they do men."[43]

Saroja, who has closely watched the experience of her sister, and through whose eyes and point of view the story of the novel unfolds itself, has had awakening of sexual knowledge through Lalitha and her friend Jaya and partly through her talks with their neighbour Manikkam's wife. Her natural desires are curbed by the strong impact of the codes of traditional society, represented by the conservative Aunt Alamelu. She also learns through Lalitha's experience where uninhibited moral freedom will land her. When she goes to the city, the presence and actions of Devraj, Mr. Gupta's assistant, disturb her. She also has erotic dreams but the realisation that presumably all men are responsible for their moral lives, prevents her own physical desires. From this insight she moves to the recognition of her own responsibility. So, when she returns to the village and Chingleput, the sweetshop vendor, in whom she had confided everything since her childhood, offers his manly blessings, she rejects him and chooses her own way of life within the bounds and restrictions of the rural society.

It is true that by the time the novel ends, Saroja has chosen to stay within the social code. Yet her own experience of life and that of her elder sister, Lalitha enable her to understand the entire scheme of relationships as they exist in this male-dominated society. She realises that the entire scheme of human relationships has been ordained by men and women have, through centuries of male-dominance, been mentally reduced to a state where they accept this arrangement as something inevitable which they have to put up with. To view this arrangement from the standpoint of a woman and to evaluate it with varying degrees of consciousness is one of the essential traits of the mental make-up of the 'new woman'. And this is what Saroja does to an extent.

In the novel Saroja looks at this scheme of things in terms of the metaphor of dominance which has the sanction of institutionalized religion. When Saroja and her family approach the city, she is filled with sympathy for the 'patient beasts' who dragged the bullock carts. The following lines make the idea very clear :

> Saroja's sympathy spurted strongly for the patient beasts, plodding along quite senselessly as far as they knew this endless road, bearing the heavy yokes on their necks. In Miss Mendoza's school, which was Christian, they taught animals were created for men, that God gave man dominion over beasts. It revolted Lalitha. She accepted a good deal but she could not accept that, she struck to her own creed, which said each creation had its own right. Men used animals, of course, but you did it with circumspection, the injunction was upon you not to encroach on their integrity. There

> were divisions in Lalitha which stemmed from her school, made her part company from Saroja whose school was differently rooted, but they came together in crucial matters like this, in basics she and Saroja and Amma and Appa were of one mind. (*TV* 192)

It is, thus, clear that so far as their perception of scheme of relationships in society is concerned, Saroja and Lalitha think alike. In the missionary school, Lalitha is told that animals are made for serving the ends of man whether as food or as beasts of burden. This dominance of man over animals, she is told by her teachers, exists because God has so dispensed it. But she is unable to accept this idea. At the concious level she attributes her rejection of the idea of dominance to her system of religious beliefs which is different. But a deeper analysis of her reaction would reveal that in the depth of her consciousness, it is not religion — neither aversion to Christianity nor adherence to her own religion — which is responsible for her reaction. It is basically the woman inside her considering this predicament as the lot of the woman where man is the dispenser, although in the incident this feeling becomes fixated to her feelings about the draught animals.

Lalitha, in her own way, tries to unsuccessfully break male-dominance through her physical beauty and charm and ultimately ends as a woman on the streets. Saroja, on the other hand, can see this metaphor of dominance in a broader perspective. The Christian belief that 'God gave man dominion over beasts' is a manifestation of the same metaphor. To the young and inquisitive mind of Saroja dawns the understanding that just as animals are for man's use, so is the plight of women in so far as man-woman relationship is concerned. She realises that in human society woman is even more disadvantageously placed than animals in this scheme of dominance. Even where men and women are equally subjected to social dominance or any other kind of dominance, men are allowed certain escape routes such as drinking, gambling, etc. This awakening comes to her when she tries to comprehend the situation of her widow aunt Alamelu :

> Aunt Alamelu had nowhere to slink to. She said it was the state her feet were in that foiled her. Saroja mulled it over, saw it was n't that at all, it was her sex. Appa and Anand (Appa's friend) could stride off to the coffee-shop, Manikkam had his bhang hide-out, Bundi's liquor-store was always crammed with men. Women had

no boltholes. There was no escape for them, they had to stand where they were and take it. (*TV* 123)

Saroja, filled with pain, looks at her own 'escape route', 'the path that led to Chingleput's sweetshop'. But such 'escape routes' are entirely personal, they have no social sanctions such as those of 'men'.

Just as a calf has a right to exist so also has an unborn child, if the mother who has conceived it wants to keep it, no matter whether it has been conceived outside wedlock or within it. Saroja, who is against any kind of dominance, even that of animals, finds the whole idea of abortion abhorring. In her case realization of dominance leads to feelings of compassion for fellow-sufferers : first it is the beasts and later on the same feeling of compassion and sympathy gets transferred to the unborn child. It shocks her sensibility to learn how a life which was taking shape in the womb was snuffed out. The two sisters discuss the whole issue after the horrifying act of abortion has been performed. In retrospect, at least, they give an inclination of their own views on the subject. When Saroja expresses her desire to know the details of abortion, Lalitha's emotional attachment to the life that was being destroyed is very touching :

> They sucked him out, said Lalitha, bit by bit. He came out in pieces. I could feel him going, though they said I would not feel anything. He would not have filled a tumbler, except for the fluid. It took ten minutes. She paused, she was hideously dry. If I had n't wanted him it might have been different she said, an unwanted child is better off unborn. But I did want him. I wanted him most when he was going, these last ten minutes of his life. (*TV* 232)

The latter part of the conversation is important in as much as it puts the whole issue in perspective :

> It's horrible, I don't want to hear, Saroja burst out. Why not said Lalitha, you are a woman, are n't you. You are n't going to slide through life untouched, you don't think?
>
> Not like this, Saroja gasped. Like what, like me? asked Lalitha. Well may be not. But you want to know, you want to know the detail of it to help you along. Did n't you? asked Saroja. She mouthed, she could n't utter.
>
> All I know it's horrible, said Lalitha, but more horrible to have gone through with it, there would have been no place for him. She

licked her blistered lips. It is n't fair she said. You would think there was some other way, would n't you? To keep a child if you wanted to, whether you were married or not? But there is n't, no way at all.

If there had been - said Saroja. Too late, said Lalitha. She smiled, she glittered, there was the sharpness of daggers about her. The thing to remember, my sweet, is never to cry over spilt milk (*TV* 232-33).

It is obvious that their sensibilities are hurt at the way life is snuffed out. They fumble for some kind of solution but there is no element of remorse for the act. Not even a word is said about the immorality of it. It is here that Lalitha becomes the 'new woman' in the real sense. She is not talking as a liberated woman; she realises that the liberated woman is a myth.

In sharp contrast to the sisters' views, we have their mother's comments which are full of the moral aspect of the act. The two sisters, on the other hand, talk entirely in a different framework - the crux of the discussion revolves around the human aspect i.e. a life being snuffed out and the entire experience of abortion. A glimpse into the mother's views enables us to see how radically different is the sister approach to the whole problem :

> You are only a child, how can you understand? said Amma. She had come back from the temple, had gone there to pray but it had brought no comfort. It's the same the world over, she said pity, there is no room for the children of *sin*. Open your eyes she begged. Saroja opened her eyes, she saw with clarity, she saw her mother's blotched face, her own was spongy with unshed tears. The *sin* is not to make room for them; she said bluntly. The *sin* is to conceive, said Amma. It is so quickly done, so easy to do ... yet who would have thought? She sat down, clasped her hands round her knees and rocked. Your sister wandered too far, she said wearily, she was lured outside the code of our community and is paying the penalty, that is all. (*TV* 234)

Kamala Markandaya discusses the issue of illegitimacy when she talks about the case of Ira in *Nectar in a Sieve* also and seems to suggest that illegitimacy is not something new. It has been there in some form or the other ever since the institution of marriage came into being. There have been rebels, too, in every kind of society — traditional or modern. But this problem of illegitimacy assumes a new dimension in *Two*

Virgins when the sisters indulge in a discussion on the subject when the abortion has been performed. There illegitimacy does n't figure as an issue - it is an issue as long as one considers its repercussions within the existing social and economic orders. But the plane of sisters' talk is independent of these social and economic orders. Therefore, in their analysis of the situation the issue is never one of illegitimacy, it is primarily a human issue — the pain and anguish that a woman has to undergo while aborting a child. The moral question is not at all mentioned. How the sisters think differently is further corroborated by Diana Trilling who considers abortion as a fictional symbol " of a deep emotional injury to a woman, a violation of the integrity of her body"[20] (517).

Commenting on the characters of these two sisters, Larson, in his perceptive commentary on the novel, says that the evolving consciousness in Saroja is a feat achieved in the third world fiction. He says, "Saroja perceives, she changes, she grows"[21] (Larson 143). This change takes place in Saroja as she witnesses the fate that befalls her sister. Contemporary Indian society is here presented as hodge-podge of traditional Indian and modern western cultures, to which Lalitha falls a victim. Modern India is shown as a country undergoing rapid social change from within and from without. The peasantry no longer knows the security of the traditional ways of life. Whatever stability there is must come from the inner strength of the individual characters. And Saroja achieves this to a great extent. Markandaya's achievement, rightly says Larson, "is to write a novel that bridges the gaps between the third world and the West : *introspective characters* strongly rooted in traditional way of life, the Indian joint family"[22] (Larson 147).

Unlike *Nectar in a Sieve* and *Two Virgins*, in *A Handful of Rice*[23] there is a male, Ravi, from whose point of view the story is narrated. Of the two main women, Nalini and Jayamma, present in the novel, it is Jayamma whose portrayal is of relevance to this study, for it is she who can be said to be possessing some of the traits of the 'new woman'. These features are driven home to us when we analyse the two planes on which the novel moves — the plane of Ravi, the protagonist and the author's own point of view which makes its appearance here and there. These two points of view lead to an incident in the novel where seeds of the 'new woman' are visible in Jayamma.

For an understanding of Jayamma, the mother-in-law of Ravi, it would be worthwhile exploring as to how the latter views the former.

Ravi, a simple lad from a village, who has come to the city in his quest for a better living, never refers to Jayamma without the use of 'animal' imagery; also he is aware of her tendency to dominate. Ravi is quick to realise that although Apu, his father-in-law, 'ran the business, who took the decisions, who held the household together', it was Jayamma, 'large and vocal', who, actually, "carried the appurtenances of strength; it was her mouse-like husband who exercised it. Ruminating on it Ravi sometimes felt affronted, indignant almost that this shrivelled-up non-entity, whom he had seen by night cowering and cringing before him, should by day order him about here and there. At these times he would wrap the jungle around him for comfort... ah yes, the jungle its darkness, its lawlessness, where a man's strength and courage alone gave him mastery ... live by jungle law and then see who survived!" (*AHR* 33).

Quite early in the novel, Ravi experiences the 'physical' toughness of Jayamma when she thrusts a coin in his hand in exchange for a menial job. "This time at least he had got under her *skin - skin*, he thought, My God, it is not *skin*, what it is hide, what they get after years and years of toughening up..." (*AHR* 25).

Jayamma's situation is also revealed to us through the author. Jayamma, who has been married to Apu, a much older man, has had an unsatisfied marriage. To this aspect of Jayamma's marital life Kamala Markandaya refers when Apu, her husband, is on his death-bed and Jayamma, like a devoted wife, nurses him: "She nursed him with the same assiduity that the doctor commended, devotedly as a wife should, out of a strong sense of duty but *without love*." (*AHR* 149).

Markandaya further elaborates :

"She had been young, he (Apu) past his prime, when they married her to him. She did not love him then, she did not love him afterward, she did not even know that she did not because she said she did not know what it meant. Suddenly she knew what love was : felt the happy delirium, the joy, the anguish, felt the yearning and strain when her arms were empty, the possessive protective passion when they were full" (*AHR* 149).

The truth of what she had been deprived of in marriage dawns on Jayamma with full force once her daughter Nalini and son-in-law, Ravi start living in the same house: "None of these things lay between her and her husband ... It was not until much later, living in the same house as the bridegroom picked for her daughter, and seeing their sated sexual faces, that she realised her other loss. She was then in the prime of her life" (*AHR* 139).

It is in such a frame of mind when Jayamma becomes actually aware of 'her other loss' that she starts associating the elements of 'dominance' and 'masculinity', which she found wanting in Apu, with Ravi. She even entertains in her mind the thought that her son-in-law is better, more masculine than her husband. So, when Ravi physically manhandles his wife Nalini, Jayamma is at first concerned for her daughter but when she realises that there are no real injuries, she holds her peace and experiences some kind of a dream fulfilment :

In all the years of their married life Apu had never once raised his hand to her, but then she thought, with the faint contempt she still bore her husband, which even his death had not expunged, in that way Apu had never been much of a man. She shivered a little thinking of Ravi's masculinity; and there was even the seed of a thought in her mind, though she would not let it grow, that in her daughter's place she would have welcomed her wounds (*AHR* 188).

Thus, the two planes of the novel- the one wherein Ravi associates Jayamma with 'animal' imagery and the other, namely, the author's view which discovers the 'seed' of Ravi's 'masculinity' in Jayamma's mind, converge in the near - incestuous encounter between the two. Ravi responds to her secret urge when he ravishes her telling her he knows her secret desire for him. The following piece of conversation between the two makes the whole point clear :

Jayamma was locking up: he could hear the bolts being rammed home. He came up behind and gripped her shoulders.

'Where is she?'

'How should I know?'

'You do.'

'I have told you I don't know. Now take your hands off me.'

'No', he said and laughed at her. 'Why should I? You 've wanted it for months, for years. All the time you lay with your husband. Every time you looked at me.'

'Ruffian. Thug.'

She was struggling. He held her and his excitement grew with her movements : her arms and breasts were soft and pulpy under his hands. 'You like it', he said, his mouth rough on her nipples, bringing them hard and erect. 'Do you think your body does n't give you away? Do you think, I know how you have been starved?'

'Gutterspine'.

But her face was luminous in the moonlight, her eyes wide and brilliant, the whites showing, closing, and he was lost, in soft enveloping flesh that tossed away past and future, wiping out pain and unhappiness, and all his waking and sleeping terrors (*AHR* 221).

What assumes significance in the whole episode is Jayamma's reaction to the incident the following morning. To Ravi's utter surprise, who is overwhelmed with 'the sin of the night bearing harshly on him', Jayamma's reaction is one of total unconcern :

'What for-last night?' she said and stared at him. 'Do you think I care about that? Who cares what goes on between four walls?' (*AHR* 223).

The aftermath of the incident is important because it gives insight into the moral aspect of the whole issue. Such incidents might be rare but they do happen in society; sometimes they are brought to light and at other times they remain hidden. But what is more important is the moral and emotional reaction of the parties involved.

Also, such incidents give rise to a number of possibilities. The persons indulging in it might derive a secret delight in enjoying something which is viewed as immoral; in such cases it would reflect the depravity of the characters. It might even become the beginning of an incestuous relationship which engulfs both the parties. In some it might give rise to feelings of self-reproach and guilt, for such individuals consider the whole thing as immoral and hence might carry its weight all their lives.

But we find no such reaction in Jayamma. She does not consider the act as immoral, nor does she consider it as something to be gloated over merely because it is illicit; it also does not become the starting point of an illicit relationship. It does not leave even an iota of mark on her psyche, much less of guilt. It is like a dream and its impact is as transitory as that of a dream. Her response is ethically neutral. This is what marks the beginnings of 'new woman' in her.

Jayamma's reaction in no way suggests that she is a rebel and hence does not care about the morality of the society she lives in. Being a member of this taboo-ridden, traditional society, she does care for its standards of morality. Here it may be recalled that in the early part of the novel she exercises immense 'vigilance' on her daughter and does not allow Ravi to meet her before marriage :

> Ravi had sisters, and so he knew the strict watch that was kept on young unmarried girls in their community, in all communities except shameless ones like the European, or, so they said, the American, or even though occasionally, among Indian Christian converts who copied their ways as well as their religion. Nevertheless it irked him unbearably to see how assiduously Jayamma glued herself to her daughter whenever he was present and unoccupied... And yet, maddening though he found Jayamma, the moral standing of the whole household— not least that of Nalini, would have fallen in Ravi's eyes had such vigilance not been exercised (*AHR* 40).

Also, Jayamma's reaction to the incident is not a defense that there is nothing wrong in this kind of relationship and hence should continue. Nor is it a plea that society should evolve in the direction where such relationships become acceptable. It is a mere acknowledgment of the fact that there are moments like this in a woman's life and if such moments do come, they should not disturb the emotional equipoise and moral balance of the woman. This is the 'new' element in Jayamma's character. And it goes entirely to the credit of the author that she is able to convert her point of view into Jayamma's and carry the reader along with her. Therein lies her success.

The 'new woman' element in Jayamma gets into a sharper focus when we analyse Ravi's reaction to the whole episode on the next day. Born and bred as he is, his sense of morality conforms to the prevalent moral norms of the society of which he is a part. Hence, as already pointed out, the sin of the previous night bears harshly on him and he begs Jayamma to forgive him. But when he discovers that the 'sin' which has weighed so heavily on his conscience has hardly affected the soul of Jayamma, it strikes his inner-self with greater sense of guilt: "The sin that stained and discoloured him was nothing to her. Invisible, so long as she was not seen committing it. No sight, no sin. Respectability, he thought, the sense of betrayal like alum on his tongue; so low, a piddling wall fit only to be kicked down" (*AHR* 233).

Here Ravi is wrong in estimating that for Jayamma it is not a sin as long as it remains 'invisible' or 'so long as she is not seen committing it'. It will be a superficial analysis. Although Jayamma utters the words, 'who cares what goes on between the four walls?', it is not her moral response. Her equipoise has roots deeper in her psyche.

In passing, it is worth mentioning that hardly any critic has cared to go deep into the character of Jayamma. Most of the critics have just described the sexual encounter between Ravi and Jayamma as nothing but incest and left at that. K. S. Narayan Rao, in his article, 'Love, Sex, Marriage and Morality in Kamala Markandaya's Novels,' published in *The Osmania Journal of English Studies* in 1973, describes the incident as "the worst of the immoral acts in the whole of Makrandaya's fictional world". In her full length analysis of women in *A Handful of Rice*, Shantha Krishnaswamy hardly devotes a line to the character of Jayamma; her preoccupation is with the description of Nalini whose "quest for autonomy (in her view) gets transformed into a protracted struggle for survival"[24] (180).

The foregoing study raises the problem faced by the 'new woman': how to reconcile such conflicting issues as illegitimacy, aborting an illegitimate child, moments of near-incest—experiences which are traumatic to a woman's being both emotionally and morally. Some believe that the 'new woman' is a rebel and through being a rebel she is able to meet such shocks. However, the 'new woman's approach to these situations is such that she does not need to be a rebel nor does she require a cushion to absorb the shock. At the core she has that moral strength which expresses itself at the surface in the form of her equipoise. Ira, Lalitha and Jayamma possess this 'equipoise' in ample measure.

The novels of Kamala Markandaya also express her feminist moral concern through in-depth investigation into sexual and familial relationships. She stresses the need to believe in the moral superiority of women in upholding the sanctity of the family. In novels such as *Nectar in a Sieve*, she presents the prohibition against loose living lest the purity of women and the stability of the home should be endangered. So, when Ira becomes a prostitute driven to it by poverty, Rukmani operates as a restrictive force. *Two Virgins*, a "novel devoted to setting before us the view of life of a sexual, moral and cultural deviate, is a feminist novel in every sense of the terrm"[25] (Geetha 133).

Kamala Markandaya here allows herself much more freedom to describe social reality for its own sake while ideological issues are played down. The portrayal of the contrasting sister-heroines is very much in the moralistic tradition of female writing. The scheme used is that of contrasted heroines, one representing female good sense and prudence, the other led into error and difficulty by impulsiveness and excesses of feeling and conduct. In this novel, which has received much critical attention, the crisis is not "the un-married woman's transgression, but the innocent girl's awakening"[26] (Geetha 134) Similarly, *A Handful of Rice* becomes a study in the 'new woman's insight into the aftermath of the moment of near-incest.

To sum up, Kamala Markandaya's novels are "metaphorical elongations of the basic fact of awakening feminine consicousness"[27] (Krishnaswamy 345). As the preceding discussion reveals, there seems to be a new awareness of fulfilments of feminine identity on social, emotional and spiritual planes, as represented by characters like Rukmani, Saroja, Lalitha and Jayamma.

There is an attempt at a reassessment of what a woman in the Indian cultural context aspires to. At the same time Kamala Markandaya does not want her characters to let go the past and their ancient heritage. This amounts to "a fundamental dualism in her novels — she tries to criticize the tradition which she has inherited, but at the same time in a sense tries to renew it"[28] (Geetha 137).

NOTES

1. H. M. Williams, "Victims and Virgins : Some Characters in Markandaya's Novels", *Perspectives on Kamala Markandaya* (Calcutta : Writers Workshop, 1976) 28.

2. P. Geetha, "The Novels of Kamala Markandaya: Reassessing Feminine Identity", *Between Spaces of Silence: Women Creative Writers* ed. Kamini Dinesh (New Delhi : Sterling, 1994) 126.

3. Sharon Spencer, "Feminist Criticism and Literature", *American Literature Today* ed. Richard Kostelanentz (Forum Series, 1982) 11, 157.

4. Geetha 127.

5. Geetha 127.

6. Shantha Krishnaswamy, *The Woman in Indian Fiction in English* (New Delhi : Ashish Publishing House, 1984) 8.

7. Kamala Markandaya, *Some Inner Fury* (London: Putman, 1955) 117.

8. Carolyn G. Heiburn, "Marriage and Contemporary Fiction", *Critical Quarterly* 5th Ser. 2 (Winter 1978) : 309.

9. Krishnaswamy 163.

10. Diana Trilling, "The Liberated Heroine", *Partisan Review* 4 (1978) : 510.
11. Kamala Markandaya, *Nectar in a Sieve* (New Delhi : Jaico Publishing House, 1992). All subsequent references to this edition will be referred to as *NS*.
12. H. S. Mahle, *Indo-Anglian Fiction : Some Perspectives* (New Delhi : Jainsons Publications, 1985) 99 - 110.
13. Bhagwat S. Goyal, *Culture and Commitment : Aspects of Indian Literature in English* (Meerut : Shalabh Book House, 1984) 108.
14. Goyal 106.
15. Goyal 106.
16. Geetha 133.
17. Kamala Markandaya, *Two Virgins* (New Delhi : Vikas Publishing House, 1977). All subsequent references to this edition will be referred to as *TV*.
18. "Colam" is a kind of traditional floor decoration generally drawn in the front yard of the house with rice - flour on religious festivals, as a sign of auspiciousness.
19. Trilling 501.
20. Trilling 517.
21. Charles R. Larson, *Fiction in Third World* (Washington, D. C. : Inscape Publishers, 1976) 143.
22. Larson, 147.
23. Kamala Markandaya, *A Handful of Rice* (New Delhi : Orient Paper-backs, 1985). All subsequent references to this edition are referred to as *AHR*.
24. Krishnaswamy 180.
25. Geetha 133.
26. Geetha 134.
27. Krishnaswamy 345.
28. Geetha 137.

4

THE 'NEW WOMAN' PROPER

Anita Desai is not a self-proclaimed or established feminist writer. As a novelist, she does not consider herself to be part of any well-defined ideological movement. Describing her art as the product of instinct, silence and waiting, she confesses that her novels do not convey any conscious philosophy. Writing, as she understands it, is not an act of deliberation, reason or choice. She claims that her novels do not even have themes -- at least till they are finished, published and read[1] (Desai, "Questionnaire"). While writing she follows her impulses and flashes of insight, veering away from, and even fighting, anything that threatens to destroy or distort this insight 2 (Ram 29). Obviously, crediting this novelist with a definite or conscious commitment to the feminist movement or to feminist ideas will be a distortion of facts. Yet there are feminist dimensions to Anita Desai's fiction and an attempt will be made to identify and study some of them.

Often hailed by critics as the first psychological novelist of India, Anita Desai is primarily concerned with characters. Her characters are neither social types nor representatives of any marginalised groups. In the course of an interview she described the kind of characters she preferred to portray as "individuals, always invariably"[3] (Srivastava 212). Her protagonists are all presented as integral selves, both men and women, struggling to define their identities in an environment that is either hostile to, or at least not in harmony with, their sensibility. She also takes care to attribute all these characters with a higher level of sensibility, which distinguishes them from the ordinary folk and makes them, at the same time, misfits in the conventional environment in which they are placed. In all her novels the focus is on their struggle; story, action and drama mean little to her except in so far as they emanate directly from the characters she writes about - are born out of their dreams, wills and actions. As a writer, she claims that a story imposed from outside, or a theme similarly imposed, may simply destroy the characters' lives and reduce them to a string of jerking puppets on a stage[4] (Desai, "Questionnaire" 4).

Further, as a novelist, Anita Desai does not believe in propagandist writing. Writing, as she says, is a process of discovery. The purpose of her writing is to discover for herself and then describe and convey the truth. And truth, as she conceives of it, is synonymous with art and not with reality[5] (Desai, "Questionnaire"1). She firmly believes that novels are not meant to illustrate theories or philosophy, although they may participate in such debates or inquiries[6] (Srivastava 222). Hence, whatever philosophical theory or ideology that can be traced to be lying concealed in between her lines, is not the subject of her deliberate explication but merely the fragments of that truth which the novelist is seeking through her writings.

Anita Desai's search for truth, through the presentation of individuals and the exploration of their psyche, has resulted in the sensitive portrayal of several interesting characters, both male and female. But a quick glance through her novels reveals that out of eight full-fledged novels that she has written so far, at least five have women as the central characters. Besides, it is evident in the observations she makes in her article on "Women Writers" that the novelist is conscious of some of the problems faced by women[7] (Desai, "Women Writers" 40). Inviting our attention to the absence of a well-defined female tradition in our written literature, she observes in this article that the literary achievements of Indian women are severely limited because of their poverty of experience and improper physical and mental Exercise[8] (Desai, "Women Writers" 41). According to Anita Desai, such a situation becomes a handicap because it directly affects their capabilities for social observation and documentation, both very important to the writing of fiction[9] (Ram 32). On another occasion, she states that women novelists necessarily (but not derogatively so) have a special way of looking at things in their works, because they live in severely confined spheres. There is no suggestion that this makes their vision inferior -- it is only different.

Anita Desai considers this essential difference in experience both as a handicap and as a privilege, for even as it restricts their field of observation, it renders it more intense. As a result, women writers place their emphasis differently from men, and have a very different set of values. Thus, while the male writers remain concerned with action, experience and achievement, their female counterparts occupy themselves with thought, emotion and sensation. The novelist later makes it clear that she does not consider this inevitable difference, and poverty of experience that causes it, as much of a drawback; she believes that a lack of sensitivity, thought, intelligence or memory would be a far greater misfortune than this[10] (Srivastava 211).

These observations reveal an important aspect of Anita Desai's outlook : she does not believe that there is any essential difference in the nature of men and women; but the limits placed on their experience and their social conditioning result in differences in their behavioural-patterns, thought and creative achievements. Evidently, whatever Anita Desai says about the creative achievements of women, also explains her own practice of creative writing. We are left with a suggestion that her works, being the creations of a woman writer, also require a different critical approach — one that is more sensitive to women's lives and women's experiences.

Like most other women writers, Anita Desai confines her novels to the inner landscape of the protagonists, delving into it with an intensity that would compensate for the limited scope of the exteriors. About her practice as a writer, she admits :

> I do restrict myself to writing about people and situations — I know or I can understand. Yes, this is the reason for my emphasis on "inner action" [11] (Srivastava 211).

Evidently, she is sticking to that "window view" and "inward turn of glance" which are the frequent resort of the female creative psyche, restricted in its experience to a domestic world.

Apart from having created a larger number of female protagonists, we notice her creative energy moulding even the male protagonists as more androgynous than 'masculine' according to conventional standards. Nirode, Adit, Deven and several of the male characters she presents in her short stories are examples. Evidence further suggests that at times she is consciously writing about problems that are unique to women. Commenting on the vitality of a male character (Raja) and the passivity of his two sisters (Bim and Tara) in one of her novels (*Clear Light of Day*), she refers explicitly to the difference in the options open to a man and a woman in Indian society. The novel is set in the late forties and the novelist says that in those days men had a different kind of life open to them which was entirely closed to girls. Girls, at that time, could not even visualise having any kind of independent will or the possibility of choosing for themselves[12] (Jain 12). During the course of another interview she talked about her response to the question of women's emancipation :

Q. You have touched upon the problem of the emancipation of women. How strongly do you believe in it and what steps do you suggest should be taken for its implementation?

A. Any statement I wish to make on the subject has been made in my novels, in one form or another. Whoever is interested in the subject will have to search for them himself[13] (Srivastava 224).

In this Study, an attempt is being made to search for this subject, namely "Women's emancipation" at a deeper level.

Anita Desai's fiction seeks to unravel the complex responses of middle-class women to their domestic world. It is a world that has web-like associations with parents, husband, siblings and children. Such a task involves confronting feminine stereotypes of Indian culture. A self-conscious writer who is aware of her difference as a female novelist, Desai employs several strategies, often within the same novel. She represents some women as moulded by social and cultural norms; such women passively suffer the limitations such norms impose. With some other women, the treatment of the author is such that "cultural formulations about gender seem to have little bearing on their subjective reality. Their problems, we are to assume, have a human dimension beyond the bounds of gender"[14] (Juneja 77). She also depicts women who consciously rebel against and reject socially-sanctioned codes of feminine behaviour. Finally, in a significant departure with *Clear Light of Day*, Desai offers women who, in "searching for autonomy, achieve independence through affirmation of some stereotypically feminine aspect of personality"[15] (Juneja 77).

Until *Clear Light of Day*, the women dominating Desai's fiction are variations of a recognizable type. They are sensitive, sometimes emotional, always misfits within their world, and struggling to preserve their integrity in the face of demands made on them. Trapped in a repressive culture or insular family, these women attempt to retain autonomy by responding in two ways : they withdraw into a subjective world, often acting in ways the society considers neurotic or mad; or they cultivate coldness or indifference, refusing to give in. With *Clear Light of Day*, a strong individualised female protagonist achieves "transcendence over inner division and social restrictions through celebration of her nurturing feminine self, through acceptance and accommodation rather than withdrawal and rejection"[16] (Juneja 77).

Shantha Krishnaswamy used the term 'abnormal consciousness' to designate the mental state of heightened receptivity experienced by the female protagonists of Anita Desai's novels. The female protagonist in each novel of Anita Desai, according to her, has that "heightened imagination and extra amount of intelligence to realise the extraordinary queerness and mysteriousness of the world in which she lives"[17] (Krishnaswamy 240). It is this awareness, this sensitivity that enables the woman of Desai to reflect on social, moral, emotional and spiritual aspects of life. And since such a reflection is a conscious one, the woman protagonist of Anita Desai earns the epithet 'the new woman' proper.

While the female protagonist of Desai thrums and quivers like a finely tuned musical instrument, her male counterpart remains stolid, glum and impervious to her finer vibrations. He is totally oblivious of her awareness, her sensitivity to external environment, both physical and mental. The tragedy in each novel, thus, can be finally traced to this disparity in sensibilities, male and female. Maya and Gautama in *Cry, The Peacock*, Sita and Raman in *Where Shall We Go This Summer?*, Nanda Kaul and her Vice-Chancellor husband in Fire On the Mountain and the majestic solitary Bimla with her cramped stuttering suitor Dr. Biswas in *Clear Light of Day* are illustrative of the incongruity inherent in such relationships.

It is the 'new woman', sensitive as she is, who is aware of the malaise in all human relationships. She tries to peel off the unwanted, the non-essential, to limit herself to the purest core of feeling; she cherishes the innermost sanctity of bare thought and wishes to rid herself of the meanness of a quotidian existence. Her extra ordinary awareness brings home with sharpness the disparity between herself and other mundane beings around her. The contradiction inherent in such a situation makes her feel that every gratification of human desire is turned either into a sin or a sickness. This consciousness brings her to the edge of emotional forbearance time and again; it becomes too intense to be borne, too painful to be ignored. She has to choose between death and a mean existence, in order to avoid being caught and rebuffed and humiliated repeatedly in the human whirlpool. Maya chooses the way out in death, Nanda Kaul shuts out all human relations, Sita compromises with bitterness while Bim, the protagonist of

Clear Light of Day, emerges from the bitterness of compromise into a visionary intuition of the continuity of life.

Cry, The Peacock [18] is the agonised cry of a woman's soul for meaning and fulfilment in life. Here, meaning and fulfilment in life have validity for a woman in terms of her own perception of these concepts. As things stand, society also does not deny that a woman has a right to fulfilment and a meaningful life. But in its view a woman can find these things through security and status. And for a married woman an understanding husband provides these essentials to meaningfulness and significance to life. It is here that a conflict in the novel starts.

Maya, the protagonist believes that meaning and fulfilment come through tenderness, mutual sharing and commitment to deeper things in life. On the other hand her husband, Gautama dismisses these feelings as childish sentiments. In his mistaken notion he thinks that Maya's doting father has gradually built up these sentiments into her mental make-up. He thinks that as a caring and loving husband it is his duty to educate Maya and lift her out of this sentimentality. He fails to perceive that Maya has not borrowed these ideas from some external agent. They are her own and they represent her deep commitment. This incapacity of Gautama represents the incapacity of the modern man and the society to understand and appreciate the emotional and spiritual needs of the 'new woman'. Although Maya, as a married woman, makes serious attempts that society, her friends, her husband's relationships — and above all feelings, yet she meets with failure. Hence, she looks for that total her husband — Gautama — should understand her fulfilment in the image of the moon which becomes the dominant metaphor in the novel.

The moon metaphor, which occurs in the novel several times, represents the life of total fulfilment at all levels of Maya's psyche. At places, it is the expression of her libido which encompasses in its range all her passions and emotions : "... there was a moon. A great moon of hot, beaten copper, of molten brass, livid and throbbing like a bloody human organ, a great, full-bosomed woman who had mounted the skies in passion, driven the silly stars away from her, while she pulsed and throbbed, pulsed and glowed across the breathless sky" (*CP* 51).

Maya does not reject this side of her psyche but the moon is also in the process of becoming as it grows from a crescent to the full moon. Through this process of becoming, the force of the libido gets softened, refined and ennobled which is again symbolised by the moon metaphor at the end of the book:

> And then we turned again, walking towards the terraced end now, and I saw, behind the line of trees that marked the horizon, the pale hushed glow of the rising moon. I held him there, while I gazed at it watching the rim of it climb swiftly above the trees, and then walked towards it in a dream of love. At the parapet edge, I paused, made him pause, and his words were lost to me as I saw the moon's vast, pure surface, touched only faintly with petals of shadow as though a great multifoliate rose, waxen white, virginal, chaste and absolute white, casting a light that was holy in its purity, a soft, suffusing glow of its chastity, casting its reflection upon the night with a vast, tender, mother love (*CP* 208).

Besides Maya, there are several other women who might be mistaken for 'new women' but a deeper analysis of their characters reveals that nearly all of them are socially emancipated and have modern outlooks but none of them possesses those attributes that would qualify them to be called 'new women' proper. The first among them is Maya's mother-in-law. She is a lady with a social commitment. Her area of social work extends to 'her dispensary or her creche, or her workshop for the blind, the disabled, the unemployed'. Unable to comprehend the problem of Maya from her pragmatic, altruistic bent of mind, she thinks Maya is just an example of 'yet another human being to be made comfortable in a hostile world.' From her point of view there is hardly any difference between Maya and 'those human beings whose comfort and health she felt responsible for.' Despite her dedication to the cause of the under privileged, the philanthropist in her is unable to perceive the deeper and hence more basic needs of the woman. Being successful and happy, she is totally oblivious of this aspect of a woman's psyche.

Another near relation of Maya who represents the modern, emancipated woman is her sister-in-law, Nila. Nila has been left by her husband after having led a married life for ten years. Now she is fighting her divorce case in a court of law. How independent she is even in matters such as divorce becomes quite evident when she comes to consult Gautama regarding her divorce. Here we are told that during an earlier family conference Gautama had refused to help his sister saying that he had nothing to do with the matter. And Nila 'in high indignation' had found herself another lawyer, on her own. When Maya comes to know of it she expresses her surprise and tells Nila, "You went *alone* and spoke to him?" (*CP* 162). To this, the independent-minded Nila replies, 'And why not? ... After ten years with that rabbit I married, I've learnt to do everything myself' (*CP* 162). Her sense of independence and responsibility is further revealed after Gautama's death when she takes up all the reins in her hands and tries to sort things out in the best possible manner. From the point of view of Maya, Nila, in spite of her wish to be on her own and lead a sensible life, does not represent the life of fulfilment. To Maya, being independent is not synonymous with leading a life of fulfilment, for fulfilment would would imply awareness of spiritual needs which Nila does not possess. Hence, she does not exemplify the 'new woman'. Maya says about these relations, "I spun around . . . to stare at my relations, whose names I knew, whose moods I sensed, whose hand I touched, and found there was not one amongst them to whom I could cry, 'Look, Look — there is a moon in the sky!' (*CP* 51).

Among her present circle of friends, there is Pom, who is modern yet a traditional woman leading a healthy, satisfied married life. In the beginning, 'the pink, plump, pretty' Pom had 'lust for newness, for brightness, colour and gaiety' and proved herself a rebel in the intial years of her marriage. She flaunted her in-laws for sometime and even forced her husband, without success, to move out of the joint family and live in an independent flat. But later on, she moulded herself and submitted meekly to her mother-in-law when the question of the birth of a son came up. She even started going to the temple. She herself disclosed this to Maya, "I'm to have a baby — in November. I take flowers to the temple every Thursday — I want it to be a boy" (*CP* 23). Pom is not aware not only of any spiritual needs but believes that a woman's happy lot is nothing beyond being rich, having a son and doing what the mother-in-law thinks proper. Maya, too, like her friend, tries to mould herself to fit in her present surroundings but this adjustment is never at the cost of her basic needs. To mould her basic needs would amount to abject surrender, which is something against her grain. For her, preserving her emotional and spiritual needs is the most important thing in life. That is why towards the end of Part II when Gautama comes between her and the moon, which symbolises for her the emotional and spiritual needs, she wishes to have him off her vision :

> And then Gautama made a mistake — his last, decisive one. In talking, gesturing, he moved in front of me, thus coming between me and the worshipped moon, his figure an ugly, crooked grey

shadow that transgressed its sorrowing chastity. 'Gautama,' I screamed in fury, and thrust out my arms towards him, out at him, into him and past him, saw him fall then, through an immensity of air, down to the very bottom. (*CP* 208)

Maya's other friend is Leila, the Persian Lecturer, who is nursing a dying husband, resigned to her fate and also to her choice. She had married him knowing that he was a patient of tuberculosis : "... He had been dying of tuberculosis when she fell in love with him, and she had married the fatality of his disease as much as the charm of his childish personality or the elegance of his dark hair falling across his white brow. When I saw her hand him a glass of medicine, or lift his body into comfortable positions, I saw in her movements an aching tenderness subdued, by a long sadness, into great beauty and great bitterness" (*CP* 57). To Maya, Leila's case appears to be a romantic impulse of love; it is not a spiritual urge and hence there are moments when she becomes vexed with herself and the husband: " 'I don't know why I rave.' She lifted one hand to her face and with four fingers, touched the centre of her forehead. 'It was all written in my fate long ago,' she said" (*CP* 59). The sensitive Maya is quick to realise that sheer sentimentality cannot become a substitute for spiritual fulfilment. Leila represents the type of woman who is a mere rebel but without any awareness of and commitment to values. Thus, Maya's friends, her relatives, her surroundings can't act as her anchor any more. That her husband, Gautama is unable to understand and appreciate her spiritual and emotional needs becomes clearer if we go a little deeper.

In the beginning we come to know that Maya's pet, Toto is dead and its death has triggered off a set of responses in her and it becomes the reason of her present misery. Although her husband makes adequate arrangements for its burial, he is unable to understand why a dog's death should perturb his wife so much.

She says : "... Oh, Gautama, pets might not mean anything to you, and yet they mean the world to me" (*CP* 16).

Gautama is unable to comprehend the genuineness and significance of the emotional and spiritual nature of Maya's feeling. To Maya, the dying moments of the pup have a deep significance. To her, the pup is the metaphor for tenderness, innocence and its death, therefore, touches the basic sympathies which lie at the core of her heart. The 'small sharp yelp' of the dying Toto is like a pebble cast into the lake of her sensibility which sets into motion waves that engulf her whole personality. For her husband, Gautama it is only the death of a pet and the episode is closed with the removal of the corpse : 'It is all over' (*CP* 6) but for Maya it is the beginning of a set of responses.

This shows a total incapacity of Gautama to fathom the depths of Maya's feelings and he, under mistaken notions, attributes her reaction to the death of the puppy as part of her growing up: she had led a protected life and has been brought up on fantasies by a doting father as "a toy princess in a toy world" (*CP* 89). He later even accuses her of living her life as a fairy tale:

> '... What have you learnt of the realities? The realities of common human existence, not love and romance, but living and dying and working all that constitutes life for the ordinary man. You won't find it in your picture-books; what wickedness to raise a child like that, ...' (*CP* 115).

How patronising, pragmatic, intelligent but without spiritual needs is Gautama becomes further evident when he and Maya discuss the case of a woman client who was pregnant and appeared in the court in this state. When Maya asks him how he felt when he looked at the woman, Gautama in a matter-of-fact-manner replies that he felt bored. Maya who feels intensely for the pregnant woman is outraged to hear this : 'You were bored? Bored? Did n't you feel anything more? Can't you feel anything except boredom. You did n't want to weep when you saw that pregnant woman. You were just bored?' (*CP* 65). But in such situations, Gautama always employs his 'cool, styptic tone' whenever he wishes to combat Maya's 'indiscipline with the sense of the practical'. He further tells her, 'Frankly if a man were to react to the sight of pregnancy by bursting into tears, Maya, no court of law would consider him sane or sober' (*CP* 65). Totally ingnorant of the import of Maya's emotional outburst and the feeling for the pregnant woman, he advises her not to grow so painfully involved.

Maya's awareness of her spiritual needs is also reflected in her attitude to the cabaret dancing girls. During one of the couple's outings with Gautama's friend, Maya goes to see a cabaret dance. Unlike the other members of the audience, she finds the dance not at all provocative, despite the vulgar display of bodies of the dancing girls through their gyrating movements. For Gautama, it is nothing but 'exhibitionism' ' as common a disease as egoism or megalomania which cannot be suppressed'. They are merely physically aberrant women of small ambition, who think it 'a compliment if men leer at their thighs.'

But Maya, whose sensitive self can see through their provocative looks and movements tells him that, 'None of them looked as though they were doing what they wanted to do. They all looked so sad to me — so terribly sad...' (*CP* 90). To Gautama's reply that they merely looked 'vapid', she tells that "they have been thrust into it by evil uncles, or stepmother - like female children in Japan who are turned into prostitutes by their own families, to earn a living for them all" (*CP* 90).

Later also, Maya is able to connect the suffering of the dancing girls with an incident in her childhood at her father's place. A bear-trainer with a bear had come to their house to give them a show of the bear's tricks. The bear was made to balance its 'tired feet' much to the delight of Maya and their gardener's five children. And when at the end of the show the poor animal was given some food by Maya, the bear-trainer expressed his anger at this. He cried, 'You have given the beast food, missahib, and not to a poor human being. If he is hungry, do I not sweat? Alas for the ignorance of the blessed rich! They will not, consider a man's hunger any more. Alas ... and rolling up his shirt, he begins to rub his belly and moan' (*CP* 88).

The whole incident left such a great impact on her sensitive self that she had a disturbed sleep that night. She had a dream which quickly dissolved into a nightmare "in which a row of soft, shaggy frailfooted bears shamble through a dance routine to the dry rattle of the tambourine. Then suddenly, behind the bears, an entire row of trainers rise up and begin to dance too, with greater vigour. They kick up their legs displaying "left feet, grin hugely and roll up their clothes and rub their bellies and bay at the moon. By a grotesque transformation, the bears are rendered into a lonely, hounded herd of gentle, thoughtful visitors from a forgotten mountain land and the gibbering, cavorting human beings are seen as monsters from some pre-historic age, gobbling and gesticulating, pointing at their genitals, turning their backs and raising their tails, with stark madness in their faces" (*CP* 89).

Thus, in Maya's dream the roles of the bear and the bear-trainer are metaphorically reversed. The single bear of the incident becomes a number of bears in the dream which represent tenderness, innocence and persecution. They are humanised. Also, the bear-trainer becomes several bear-trainers representing voilence, lust and greed. They are brutalised. Through these images the 'new woman' in Maya perceives the roles of a sensitive and suffering woman and an unfeeling, pragmatic and dominant man in society.

The episode of the bear of Maya's childhood and that of the cabaret dancers which she sees during married life later become integrated when viewed in totality. She draws a parallelism between the bear dance and the cabaret dance and also between the bear owner and the audience that views the cabaret. The bear appears to Maya as a hungry persecuted creature — even the little food that it got was grudged by the owner. At night also in her dream, the bear appeared to her a persecuted being. In the same way, when the cabaret dance ends and somebody switches the light on, the audience appears to her nothing but bear-dancers and the devils which she had seen in the dream and the girls as the persecuted ones. Thus, Maya, with her sensibility, is able to identify her suffering through the mataphor of persecution.

Maya also compares herself to the peacocks who mate only after fighting : "When they have exhausted themselves in the battle, they will mate. Peacocks are wise. The hundred eyes upon their tails have seen the truth of life and death and know them to be one. Living, they are aware of death. Dying they are in love with life. 'Lover, Lover,' you will hear them cry in the forests when the rain clouds come, Lover, I die' " (CP 95-96). What she says about the peacocks is what she believes of what she has heard about them. But the significant thing is the 'cry' and the 'cry' is also a metaphor which stands for ecstasy, sharing, companionship which alone mean fulfilment and it is for this that she yearns.

Quite early in the novel, soon after Toto's death, Maya emphasizes the importance of closeness and bodily contact with her husband : "And so we strolled up and down the lawn, talking desultorily, not really listening to each other, being intent, on our own paths which, however, ran parallel and closely enough for us to briefly brush against each other, now and then, reminding us — or perhaps only myself — of the peace that comes from companion life alone, from brother flesh. Contact, relationship, Communion ... I let these warm, tender sensations bathe me in the lambency, soothe me till the disturbed murmurs of my agitation grew calmer, and I could step out of the painful seclusion of my feelings into an evening world where the lawn had just been trimmed, the flower-beds just watered" (*CP* 18). Being in search of 'contact, relationship, communion' she leans from person to person in the novel but without success: "There was not one of my friends who could act as an anchor any more, and to whomsoever I turned for reassurance, betrayed me now" (*CP* 18).

All that Maya desires is love from a person who is capable of loving. In other words, she wants that this kind of love should come from a person who can cherish companionship and share the same moral and spiritual experiences with her. Maya has a glimpse of this kind of love when they are driving back home after a party: "... I remembered, how, as we had driven home down a dark street I had seen a dark woman in a crimson sari, holding a white dog on a leash, walk into a shuttered house, followed by a dark young man in white. At the door, she paused, turned and smiled at him, and he smiled in reply, and went up the steps behind her, The white dog, unsmiling followed them in, and we swept past and away even before the door had shut behind them" (*CP* 94).

What Maya sees is only a moment's fleeting vision but the moment embodies all the elements which she seeks in love and in marriage — a feeling of tenderness, understanding, sharing and companionship. Gautama, on the other hand, can only offer her security, patronage, comfort, intellectual guidance and at times indulgence. Her quest is for a deeper meaning in husband-wife relationship. The meaning is realised only when the emotional and spiritual needs of a woman get recognition in marital relationship instead of the socially accepted ones of security, comfort and respectability.

The structure of the novel enables us to visualise Maya from two entirely different points of view. The brief first part is her husband's point of view and the equally brief third part is Maya's sister-in-law's point of view. As a practical woman, Maya's sister-in-law took charge of the situation after Gautama had fallen to his death when Maya had pushed him aside from the terrace. Nila, with admirable practical skill had saved the family from shame and loss of fame which would have followed the incident.

The long second part between the brief first and the third part is, therefore, like viewing Maya from a pragmatic and matter-of-fact point of view. According to this point of view, Maya's case is that of a morbid personality ending up in insanity. This seems logical enough if we accept the points of view of the first and the third part as reliable. Then, Maya's talk of tenderness, understanding, sharing, feeling, commitment are the sentimental expressions of a sickly mind which refuses to grow up and face the light. Symbolically, this is the incapacity of the pragmatic approach to fathom the depth of the 'new woman's psyche, for this approach measures everything in terms of success.

But there is another point of view, that of Maya, where it is commitment that matters. Maya was unsuccessful (to an extent) and frustrated and the trauma of frustration was as violent as her urge and the spiritual needs, which were the prime movers of her personality, were overpowering. However, it should not detract us from evaluating whether these motivating forces and her emotional urge and spiritual needs were pointless.

Here it may be mentioned that the trauma is not against mankind or male-chauvinism. Modern women can take up different forms. In the novel itself we have the example of Maya's mother-in-law who is a social reformer. Then there is her sister-in-law who is fighting her divorce petition in a court of law after ten years of married life and thus trying to be on her own. Also, we have her friend Leila, the Persian lecturer, who has married a tubercular patient purely for love and finally there is Pom, modern yet traditional woman who surrenders before her mother-in-law when the question of the birth of a son comes up and starts going to the temple to achieve this end. All these paradigms are there but they remain at the periphery of Maya's personality; none of them reaches the core of her personality. Her deep-rooted urge to realise the fulfilment of her emotional and spiritual desires remains unfulfilled although she makes sincere efforts. Therefore, her mental condition results in nothing but insanity. It might be Maya's failure bringing about her insanity but her insanity does not invalidate her urges for emotional and spiritual needs.

As in *Cry, The Peacock,* Sita, the protagonist of *Where Shall We Go This Summer?,* too, looks for a life of fulfilment but is unable to achieve this end in the marital context. For her, fulfilment implies appreciation of her tender, delicate feelings and emotions and a throbbing live of consiousness and as such what she demands is a sensitive approach in others towards herself. She realises that a cruel and insensitive environment would not provide this. This includes her immediate environment, namely, her husband and her children. Judged from the point of view of society Sita has everything — a happy domestic life where her physical and maternal needs are being met. But what Sita finds in this dull tedium of domestic life is meaninglessness. Hence, in order to avoid this, she resorts to 'escape' in the earlier part of the novel. And when she actually resorts to 'escape', she comes out with a new awareness of her situation and also of the various relationships that go with it. It is not that the 'new woman' in her has moulded herself to suit her environment. Her basic needs remain the same but after the 'escape' she returns with a new perception, a new understanding.

Sita is over forty and is awaiting the birth of her fifth child. She has realised the futility of her attempts at reconciliation between the two levels of existence which she has been living. At one level she is a wife and a mother. But she is also a person and a woman. She discovers that in the frame of reference determined by the society she cannot be a wife and a mother without surrendering her existence as a person and as a woman. Therefore, in the earlier part of the novel she decides that to achieve fulfilment as a person and as a woman she must reject her role as a wife and a mother and return to the Manori island where she can find fulfilment as a woman and as a person.

She finds that the world around her is exulting in destruction. She views her position through the metaphor of violence. According to Sita, her husband and children thrive in a world where wanton and cruel destruction is the main element and creation is something which is considered a freak or a temporary doomed existence. So much so that she even questions whether child-birth is an act of creation or a violent pain stricken act that destroys everything what is safely contained in the womb by releasing it into a murderous world. At each act of unthinking violence — her boys fighting a duel like heroes in the films, her daughter Maneka wantonly ripping the buds of a plant or tearing her paintings, and her youngest son, Karan demolishing his toys with Karate blows, Raman munching his breakfast while she tries desperately to frighten away the crows who are bent upon killing a fallen eagle — she recoils and withdraws into herself.

But her husband, Raman cannot understand the expression of fear, rage and revolt 'of a woman in her forties, greying, aging to behave with such a total lack of control'. He stands silent and blind in his disbelief. All he says is, 'Don't be silly,' 'Sita, don't behave like a fool,' 'think of your condition,' 'you've gone mad.' These expressions of his distaste towards her emotional outbursts further trigger more outbursts on her part.

It is not only the complacency and the violence of the life arround her but also the voilence in the world at large that disturbs her:

> They all hammered at her with cruel fists —the fallen blocks, the torn water-colours, the headlines about the war in Vietnam, the photograph of women weeping over a small grave, another of a crowd outside a Rhodesian jail; articles about the perfidy of

Pakistan. They were hand-grenades all, hurled at her frail gold-fish-bowl belly and instinctively she laid her hands over it (*WSWGTS* 55).

The destruction around her overwhelms her and she goes to Manori in search of a miracle. She has a notion that if she can somehow succeed in keeping the unborn child within the womb itself, it would protect him from a cruel environment; it is her way of continuing and preserving life without the need for it to be exposed to constant danger. It is also a desire to find a meaning for existence :

> Physically so resigned, she could not inwardly accept that this was all there was to life, that life would continue thus inside this small, enclosed area with these few characters churning around and then past her, leaving her always in this grey, dull-lit empty shell (*WSWGTS* 54).

The trip to Manori is actually a trip back to her childhood. Life at Manori for her had assumed some kind of perfection because it had ceased to be. But this trip becomes for her a trip of self-discovery and a recognition of reality

Sita's return to Manori is not undertaken under any illusion that she would be able to relive her life as she had done as a child. While still on the island, as a young girl, she had slowly but surely outgrown the magic spell cast during her childhood, and she had begun to question. She had struggled to free herself from the mesmerizing personality of her father but now after twenty years, the island again gains prominence in her life. The island becomes a metaphor of escape: "Knowing that, accepting that, she knew it was because ordinary life, the every day world had grown so insufferable to her that she could think of the magic island again as of release" (*WSWGTS* 101).

Sita's withdrawal is indicative of her great need for love, the kind of free, unquestioning love which would envelop her. As an example of this love she narrates to Raman a scene that she had observed of a young woman dying of tuberculosis and being devotedly attended to by a person who loved her. To Sita, it is her own brief vision of perfect harmony between a man and a woman. She tells Raman :

> Near a tall hedge, on a bench, I saw a woman stretched out. A Muslim woman. She was wrapped up in her black burkha. Then she raised her veil and I saw her face ... lying in those black folds like a flower — a dead-white flower ... A very young woman, very

pale and beautiful ... fatally anaemic — or fatally tubercular ... Her head .. lay in the lap of an old man. Much much older than her ... He looked down at her and caressed her face — so tenderly... the man and the woman never looked at any one else, they looked at each other with a strange, strange expression ... Tender, loving eyes — but inhumanly so ... One does not see such an expression on human faces ever. Quite divine — or insane ... she was ill, dying perhaps ... They were like a work of art — so apart from the rest of us (*WSWGTS* 106) .

This kind of love transcends the self and makes no claims. It is a love in the face of death, the ultimate human reality. It is this kind of relationship which she wants from Raman but which she is unable to achieve. Her distress at the tedium of a blank meaningless life does not bother him — he is hardly aware of the basic aspects of her emotional life. There is a total lack of communication between husband and wife. Commenting on the scene of lovers in the park, Nimmie Poovaya says :"The images Sita uses to describe this relationship are significant — 'anaemic,' tubercular', 'dead-white', 'dying' etc. ... Sita cannot help imbuing the image of the couple with an atmosphere of transitoriness and death"[20] (Poovaya 210 -11).

At the overt level these are images suggestive of sickness and death but what Sita sees deeper inside is mutually shared love and understanding. It is the perception of this feeling at the core which makes the incident so significant in Sita's consiciousness.

The perception of sickness at the periphery but love at the core helps Sita to attempt to re-orient her attitude to the people around her. The first step in this direction is to come out of the shadow of her father's influence, for in order to be herself she wants to share this new-island. She says to him, "My father's dead — look after me" (*WSWGTS* 131).

But her husband's inability to comprehend the feelings of his wife again make it difficult for her to start a new life with him. She has grown out of her earlier obsession but her husband and the people around her have yet to do so. She sees them "like larvae in stiff spun cocoons" (*WSWGTS* 131).

Sita yearns for a life of fulfilment and happiness —she has seen it in the glimpse of the sick couple but her husband and the society measure happiness in terms of achievement, not in terms of fulfilment. There is an incompatibility between the two approaches. What Sita means by happiness is in her husband's view morbidity while in Sita's view what the society thinks of happiness is shallow sentimentality: "What other women call happiness is just, just sentimentality" (*WSWGTS* 107). She is an honest being who is willing to face issues, who refuses all attempts to dam her sensitivity.

Women have been traditionally brought up to regard motherhood as the highest fulfilment of womanhood. But Sita questions this and she is serious and sincere in questioning this role which women have been taught to accept. She frankly tells Raman, "Children only mean anxiety, concern, pessimism, not happiness" (*WSWGTS* 107). Yet she comes to realise through her conscious reflection on these problems that 'escape' is not the answer and she decides to return to Bombay for the birth of her child, for 'escape' would be cowardly. She tells Raman: "No, — desertion, that's cowardly. I was n't doing anything cowardly," she begged him to see, with a turbulence of pride. "I was saying No — but positively, positively saying No. There must be some who say No, Raman!" (*WSWGTS* 48-49).

To Sita, protest and dissent are not cowardly acts. She, who is so sensitive to suffering all around her, has to gear herself to bear another new-born launch its life with a scream. She sees in her mind's eye the gynaecological ward, with its impassive bored nurses, bored by yet another woman in labour assisting in childbirth which she had tried to avoid, the birth she had run away from in fright and disgust. Her sojourn at Manori has, however, given her a new awareness. She realises now, "What a farce marriage was, all human relationships" (*WSWGTS* 105).

Sita's decision to return to her husband, in no sense, signifies her failure. On the contrary, it suggests that she has learnt patience and courage to face life with all its ups and downs. Her struggle symbolises "the intelligent and sensitive woman's revolt against the male smugness and philistinism trampling all finer values in marital life"[21] (Asnani 66).

Viewed from a feminist point of view Sita achieves "personhood" but does not negate family or society. She goes beyond what Elaine Showalter calls the "female phase" which is "a phase of *self-discovery*, a turning inward freed from the dependency of opposition, a search for identity"[22] (Showalter 13). With this superior knowledge she tries to re-integrate herself into the second: "The second stage cannot be seen in terms of women alone, our separate personhood or equality with men. The second stage involves coming to new terms with the family — new terms with love and with work"[23] (Friedan 13).

Her perception of her husband and society have not undergone any change. Sita's return from the island to Bombay and to her husband and her family is not the Prodigal Son's return—the son who returned because he wanted to be accepted. Sita returns not because she thinks that to be 'accepted' is significant to a woman. She returns because she has learnt that in spite of the attitude of society the 'new woman' must not escape from it.

In *Fire On the Mountain*[24] we find barrenness as the dominant metaphor. All the important characters —Nanda Kaul, Ila Das and even the girl -- child, Raka — fit into the metaphor of barrenness. In this context the history of the lodge, Carignano, where Nanda Kaul has come to stay in her old age, too, becomes relevant because it also contributes to the metaphor of barrenness. It is a story in which the attempt to escape barrenness brings destruction. Ultimately barrenness sucks everything into its wortex.

The main character, Nanda Kaul has been the Vice Chancellor's wife and she has performed her duties in keeping with this status. "Draped in silk sarees, she has presided over his table and managed her household. She had sufffered from "the nimiety, the disorder, the fluctuating and unpredictable excess" (*FM* 30). But even in the midst of this busy life, she had tried to fortify and steady herself by an hour of stillness every day:

> She had practised this stillness, this composure for years, for an hour every afternoon : it was an art not easily acquired. The most difficult had been those years in that busy house where doors were never shut, and feet flew, or tramped, without ceasing. She remembered how she had tried to shut out sound by shutting out light, how she had spent the sleepless hour making out the direction from which a shout came, or a burst of giggles, an ominous growling from the dogs, the spray of gravel under bicycle wheels on drive, a contest of squirrels over the guavas in the orchard, the dry rattle of eucalyptus leaves in the sun, a drop, then spray and rush of water from a tap. All was subdued, but nothing was ever still (*FM* 23).

It would be wrong to assume that she enjoyed her role as an involved woman performing the functions of a mother and a wife. To her, all relations have remained at the periphery. Living in this mountain retreat of Kasauli, liberated from the duties of wifehood and motherhood, "she revelled in its barrenness, its emptiness" (*FM* 31). She wished to "be a charred tree trunk in the forest, a broken pillar of marble in the desert, a lizard on a stone wall she would imitate death like a lizard" (*FM* 23). She treasures her freedom, her privacy, glad her responsibilities towards her family are over, glad that she needs nobody now and nobody needs her. Now she has old age and retirement to contemplate upon : "She had suffered from the nimiety, the discorder, the fluctuating and unpredictable excess". She had been glad when it was over. She had been glad to leave it all behind, in the plains, like a great heavy difficult book that she had read through and was not required to read again" (*FM* 30).

Nanda Kaul lives alone with a single servant, keeps the large rooms practically bare (except for one image of Buddha in repose) and has never bothered to plant a single fruit tree or flowering shrub on her grounds to add to the three apricot trees and rose bushes left by the previous tenant.

For a woman living alone after a hectic life, "Nanda Kaul does not seem to suffer any feelings of protest, regret or emptiness"[25] (Parasuram 60). In fact, she is happy to be left alone — left alone to the pines and cicadas which constantly make their presence felt in the natural world around her. She is aware of the different moods and changes of the natural elements, the aspects of wind, the sun during the changing hours of the day, the colours of flowers in changing seasons, and the habits of birds that have their nests in the apricot trees. But she would n't like to be involved seriously with other human beings, visits no one and does not even like to receive letters which to her are intrusions into her quiet life. "Is it wrong" she thinks in a mood of self-scrutiny, "Have I not done enough? I want no more. I want nothing, can I not be left with nothing?" (*FM* 17). The sense of detachment she has consciously cultivated to guard and preserve herself from a continued attachment to the world almost smacks of the religious ideal in the Gita of which we get many references in the earlier works of Desai "Women in those novels had wondered at the possibility of that delicate poise between carefully controlled detachment and attachment and longed for such a state to effect liberation from amorphous passions. Nanda in this book tries to remain above her past involvements and practises a controlled poise which gives her a sense of daring, independence and integration of personality" (Parasuram 61).

But stillness eludes Nanda even at Carignano also although she wants to hold on to it and be left alone with herself. Obviously, it is not possible. Claims continue to be made on her. By arriving at Carignano she had not been able to do away with the act of living. The postman brings letters, the telephone rings and before she is aware her great-grand daughter, Raka descends on her. "To Nanda Kaul she was still an intruder, an outsider, a mosquito flown up from the plains to tease and worry" (*FM* 40).

Raka's arrival at Carignano is a threat to Nanda Kaul's consciously guarded 'privacy'. She hates the nasty thought of 'opening of that old, troublesome ledger again'. She finds it painfully difficult to re-enter the business of living. Her deep agony is delineated poignantly: Hanging her head miserably, it seemed too much to her that she should now have to meet Raka, discover her as an individual and, worse, as a relation, a dependent. She would have to urge her to eat eggs and spinach, caution her against lifting stones in the garden under which scorpions might be asleep, see her to bed at night and lie in the next room, wondering if the child slept, straining to catch a sound...

She would never be able to sleep, Nanda Kaul moaned to herself, how could she sleep with someone else in the house, it would upset her so (*FM* 35).

For a while Nanda tries to shut people out; she does not pay attention to Raka : She postpones her childhood friend, Ila Das's visit to Carignano. In all this she meets with a measure of success until she is drawn out of herself by Raka's withdrawal, and sees in it some semblance to her own. Raka seems to have no need for human company. "Mostly she saw no one. She had the gift of avoiding what she regarded as dispensable" (*FM* 63). Raka makes no demands on her great-grand mother, for she has no needs. She has mastered the technique of existing and yet appearing non-existent. She explores the ravines where jackals prowl, she goes on unknown and mysterious expeditions on her own and she broods silently over the strange landscape and the fantastic and improbable things she sees. She seems to be totally absorbed in a world of her own and ignores Nanda Kaul with a "total rejection, so natural, instinctive and effortless" when compared with Nanda's "planned and wilful rejection of the child. "... If Nanda Kaul was recluse out of vengeance for a long life of duty and obligation, her great-grand daughter was a recluse by nature, by instinct. She had not arrived at this condition by a long route of rejection and sacrifice, — she was born to it simply" (*FM* 48).

It is this attitude of Raka that perturbs Nanda Kaul. She wishes to come out of her shell of barrenness and penetrate Raka's secret world. "She could not tell why she wanted to bring Raka out in the open. It was not how she herself chose to live. She did not really wish to impose herself, or her ways, on Raka. Yet she could not leave her alone" (*FM* 63). She offers to go for walk with her and during this walk, "there is a moment of shared laughter, a coming together as it were only to pull apart the moment the idea of pattern enters their conversation" (*FM* 58 -59). Raka's sense of the essential upsets Nanda Kaul and her withdrawal does not appear to be something normal. Nanda Kaul desires a response from her. She seeks to fire her imagination in order to hold her interest, in the process she endows her father with imaginary travels, travels which he had never undertaken and with animals he had never kept. Thus, she finds herself slowly getting involved in Raka and she is overcome by a strange desire to hold on to the child. "Somehow she could not bear to let her slip away. It was as if Raka's indifference was a goad, a challenge to her — the elusive fish, the golden catch" (*FM* 143).

While Nanda Kaul is making a desperate bid to enter Raka's secret world, her childhood friend, Ila Das visits Carignano. Ila Das exemplifies the opposition which a woman social worker has to face in a male dominated society. Her exposure to violence and brutality which ultimately results in her death illustrates this. Hers is an example of a woman who really wished to change the society. She is quite different from Maya's mother-in-law who also talks of social work but operates in a safe zone.

Ila Das is an example of woman's courage and strength when confronted by male dominance in terms of inheritance and education which perpetuate dependency. From her own experience, Ila Das realizes the importance of an education that will prepare women for the world outside home and the need for women to look after their own well-being. By challenging male authority, Ila Das espouses the feminist cause through her conscious need to empower men. Rather than becoming angry and destructive, she, as a social worker, tries to restructure the lives of the poor and oppressed village women. Ila Das feels that it is necessary to "shoulder our responsibility and do what we can" (*FM* 130). "As a heroine and a feminist, Ila Das combines energy, determination, and courage to protest male-dominance which relegates women to positions of subservience and submission"[27] (Rosenwasser 102).

At one stroke Ila Das's death rips the curtain aside for Nanda Kaul and the hideous reality is revealed:

> It was all a lie, all. She had lied to Raka, lied about everything... Nor had her husband loved and cherished her and kept her like a queen — he had only done enough to keep her quite while he carried on a life-long affair with Miss David, the Mathematics mistress, whom he had not married because she was Christian but whom he had loved, all his life loved. And her children — the children were all alien to her nature. She neither understood nor loved them. She did not live here alone by choice — she lived here alone because that was what she was forced to do, reduced to doing. All those graces and glories with which she had tried to captivate Raka were only a fabrication. They helped her sleep at night, they were tranquilisers, pills. She had lied to Raka. And Ila had lied too, Ila too, had lied, had tried (*FM* 145).

Thus, both Nanda Kaul and Ila Das try to escape their shells of barrenness by fabrication of a fantasy. Ila Das dies living her fantasy while Nanda Kaul, unable to bear the reality any more, dies too of choking. Raka, who understands the hollowness of the fantastic world created for her by these two women, releases herself from this whole barrenness-stricken environment by setting fire to the mountain. Unable to give verbal expression to this state, it is a sensitive child's way of reacting to the whole situation.

A deeper analysis into the consciousness of Nanda Kaul would reveal her approach to life and the relationships that go with it. All her life she has successfully performed the role of a wife, mother, daughter, grand-mother and even great-grandmother, yet none of these relationships could reach the core of her personality. Viewed from the point of society, her multifarious roles as mother, wife, daughter, etc. would be judged commendable and Nanda Kaul labelled a successful woman in worldly terms. In this context, even her putting up with her husband's life-long affair with the Christian Mathematics teacher would be lauded by the society, yet this betrayal on the part of her husband does not touch her inner being at all; like other relationships, this, too, remains shut out. Similarly placed women in society who put up with their husband's betrayal still cherish the desire that the latter return to them after sometime or enliven their lives through occasional favorable gestures. But no such yearning or desire ever crops up in Nanda Kaul's mind — she just considers the whole thing meaningless.

The foregoing analysis about Nanda Kaul's mind enables us to understand her character in perspective. The 'new-woman' in her is perhaps trying to discover whether anything else exists beyond the matrix of her relationships as wife, mother, daughter, etc. These relationships which serve as indices of fulfilment for a woman, have become totally meaningless for her. All she has discovered is barrenness and she revels in it. The moment she tries to worm herself into any kind of relationship she fails and that is what happens in her relationship with Raka. She tries to create a jocund and joyous world for Raka but fails. Thus, for Nanda Kaul the compromise between external and inner experience is something which is makeshift and senseless.

As a passing reference, it may also be mentioned that certain critics have tried to discover existentialist overtones in Desai's *Fire on the Mountain*. Nanda Kaul's state of 'aloneness' is not in the sense of existential alienation wherein individual gets alienated from the people of the world. In her case this 'aloneness' is of her own making and she has practised this even while discharging her worldly duties. What she has desired all along is negation, i.e. shutting out herself from others. In other words, she seems to be saying, "I don't want anyone". This negation, thus, implies affirmation which would amount to her stating simply, "I don't want anyone". This negation, thus, simply, "I want to be alone". Thus, Nanda Kaul's existentialist approach is of negation-affirmation type for which she owns full responsibility and does not shift the blame on either any individual or society. Hence, "existentialism as a philosophy of revolt against the unimpeded encroachment of society on the self of the individual"[28] (Khanna 130) does not hold good in the case of *Fire On the Mountain*, for it gives no indication of any such revolt on the part of the protagonist.

Clear Light of Day[29] centres around a house in old Delhi. The house itself is a metaphor. It is like a shell enclosing within its four walls the inmates who have grown up there. They are the two sisters, Bim and Tara and their alcoholic aunt, Mira Masi. All of them need some kind of a protective shell which can encase them and protect them from the various stresses and strains.

One of the brothers Baba is mentally retarded and does not involve himself into anything worthwhile except winding up his old gramaphone and listening to the records of the forties. Nearly for all his needs, he is totally dependent on his elder sister Bim. Mira Masi's case is no different. With nothing to look forward to, Mira Masi remains confined to the house 'swigging secretly from her brandy bottel.' For both Baba and Mira Masi there is nothing beyond the world of their own house. Raja, the elder brother, is intelligent and sensitive and from the beginning wishes to be different from his brother and sisters. His interest in poetry which begins as a hobby becomes an obsession with him. It even earns him the epithet of 'Lord Byron' from his friends in college. His model is their neighbour, Hyder Ali Sahib at whose residence he spends most of his evenings participating in Urdu poetry recitals. This is actually his world of make-believe. It becomes for him some kind of a psychological shell into which he can withdraw in order to escape from the shadow of the house which to him is a circumscribing shell. Thus, Raja is inside a double-shell — the protective house and his own world of make-believe. He escapes from one shell — the house only to be encased in another shell — the world of make-believe.

But it is when we come to the two women characters, the two sisters Bim and Tara that the metaphor of the house as an enclosing shell assumes significance. The younger sister, Tara remains in this shell only so long as she needs protection. As soon as she meets Bakul, a foreign service officer, she realises that now she does not need the protection of the old house. She marries Bakul and sets up a household of her own. But in the case of the main character Bim, the elder sister, the house becomes on obsession, she refuses to consider the house as a protective shell. On the other hand, she takes it as an essential and inalienable part of her personality and also of all those connected with it. They are her brothers Raja and Baba, her sister, Tara and aunt, Mira Masi. Leaving the house would be like splitting one's personality. She becomes so obsessed with it that she considers every thing as evil and detestable which leads the inmates of the house to break away from it. The most significant of these things is marriage, especially for women. They grow up, fall in love, get married and leave the house in a natural manner. Therefore, to Bim, marriage is evil. This gives rise to her differences with her sister, Tara and these differences come into sharp focus with Tara's visit to the house after several years.

Tara recollects the days of her childhood when both Bim and Raja would make fun of her. When challenged to answer the question on what she would like to be on growing up, Tara, much to the amusement of Raja and Bim, chooses to be a mother. Yet she is the first to move out of the protective shell of the house, she is the only one who realises what she had set out to do, however, imperfect her model might have been. Here is the difference between the two sisters :

> Bim, of course, worshipped Florence Nightingale along with Joan of Arc in her private pantheon of saints and goddesses and Tara did not tell her that she hoped never to have to do anything in the world, that she wanted to hide under Aunt Mira's quilt or behind the shrubs in the garden and never be asked to come out and do anything, prove herself to be anything (*CLD* 126).

Since Tara does not have anything in her mind to 'prove herself', she finds marriage as the only alternative to escape the shell-like atmosphere of the house. But for Bim the very mention of the word 'marriage' triggers off a violent response. This becomes clear when the two sisters discuss the issue of the marriage of their neighbour, Mishra's daughters. The following piece of conversation is important from this point of view :

> 'Why? repeated Bim indignantly. 'Why because they might find marriage isn't enough to last them the whole of their lives, she said darkly, mysteriously. 'What else could there be? counterd Tara. 'I mean', she fumbled, 'for them'. 'What *else?*' asked Bim. 'Can't you think? I can think of hundreds of things to do instead. I wont marry', she added, very firmly.
>
> Tara glanced at her sideways with a slightly sceptical smile.
>
> 'I won't,' repeated Bim, adding 'I shall never leave Baba and Raja and Mira Masi',... "I shall work - I shall do things', she went on, ' I shall earn my own living — and look after Mira Masi and Baba and — and be independent. There will be so many things to do— when we are grown up — when all this is over —? (*CLD* 140-41).

Here it may be mentioned that what Bim says about 'marriage' cannot be termed Bim's attitude to marriage as such. In her view, since marriage is the only means which makes the inmates of the house leave it, the very idea of marriage is detestable. If there had been anything else other than marriage that would have compelled the inmates to leave the house, Bim would have even opposed that. Hence, Bim's views are not against the institution of marriage as such. Viewed in the context of her obsession with the house, they acquire an altogether different meaning.

Tara's visit also turns out to be an occasion when Bim goes down memory-lane and relives the resentment and bitterness that she has nurtured against her brother Raja. For twenty years Bim has tormented herself with the rejection, the desertion of Raja who was an ideal for her and whom she considered only worth loving. It was a love based on sharing and understanding. As Raja runs away to Hyder Ali in Hyderabad, leaving her in the crumbling house with an alcoholic aunt and a mentally retarded brother, leaving her to manage finances and carry on, her bitterness feeds on her rejection and alientation. As in the case of Tara, in Raja's case too, it is marriage that takes him out of the house never to return. In Hyderbad Raja marries their earlier neighbour Hyder Ali's daughter, Benazir. Through this marriage Raja has come out of both the encasing shells—the house as well as the poet's world of make believe. He has become free and also pragmatic. This change in his mental make-up is reflected in the letter he sends to Bim informing her that he has inherited Hyder Ali's entire property and he assures her that she could stay in the house as long as she wants and that he would never dream of increasing the rent or asking her to vacate the house. For Bim, Raja, whom she had idealised, has stooped so low and has become so matter-of-fact snapping all the emotional ties that had ever existed between the two. She feels humiliated and insulted by such a letter. She goes on building her resentment against him, finding fault with everything Raja does. And when Raja, sensing her attitude towards him, writes letters to the younger sister Tara with whom he had never been close, Bim thinks in her spite that they have all turned their backs on her.

It is quite important to be mentioned here that Bim's obsession with the house is not entirely of her own making — it is also necessitated by circumstances. We come to know that Bim was better endowed in every way than her other brothers and sisters. She was the Head Girl at the school and wanted to be a heroine like Florence Nightingale and Joan of Arc but the untimely death of her parents and the neglect of the family responsibility on the part of Raja forces her to stay in the same place and follow the same dull routine. She lives in the house she was born, teaches in the college where she was taught and her world has shrunk to the boundaries of the house and her companion is just Baba. These forces have so warped her personality that she begins to consider the circumscribing nature of the house as something ideal and because of this warped vision she sees everyone who struggles to get free of the house as her enemies. Bim and Baba can be compared to "larvae in stiff spun cocoons" (*WSWGTS* 131) and Bim refuses to come out of this 'cocoon-house'. The larvae, in order to form into a butterfly, must break the 'cocoon' and come out.

And for Bim to become the 'new woman', she must break the barriers of her circumscribing mentality and 'come out'. This would imply her acceptance of those who had moved out of the 'cocoon house', namely, her brother Raja and sister Tara.

Tara's presence also becomes the catalyst in helping Bim to 'come out'. The occasion is provided by an event that demands immediate attention. Bim is required to sell the family insurance business. This calls for outside help — a help that she can get only from outside the 'house'. Bim, for whom the house had hitherto been a self-sufficient entity requiring no external help, suddenly finds herself incapable of handling such a situation. In one go all the presumptions fall. Unable to handle this alone, in her helplessness she tries to have her spite on Baba -- poor Baba sits helplessly dangling his loose arms withdrawn from her as if she had slapped him and them quietly goes to sleep.

Baba could neither sulk nor wish to punish her. He knows neither grudge nor punishment. It is Baba's peaceful sleep which makes Bim see the clear light of day. She realises :

> How she loved him, loved Raja and Tara and all of them who had lived in this house with her. There could be no love more deep and full and wide than this one, she knew. No other love had started so far back in time and had so much time in which to grow and spread . . . Nor was there any one else on earth whom she was willing to forgive move readily or completely or defend more instinctively and instantly. (*CLD* 165).

This is the moment in Bim's life when the 'new woman' in her breaks the 'cocoon' and 'comes out'. Though she does not go out of the 'cocoon-house,' in this new insight she is liberated from the circumscribing mentality. For her, the house does not remain a 'cocoon', anymore. With this new insight, she accepts those who had moved out. She realises that Raja, Tara, Baba — they are all parts of her. Together they form the perfect whole. And if one of them were missing, its perfectness would be gone. It occurs to her that she is the same length as Baba and if she lies herself down beside him, his slightness would mould together with her convexities. Together they would form a whole that would be perfect and pure. Somehow she would have to forgive Raja for that unforgivable letter. Silent tears fall down the sides of her face and she feels peace descend upon her heart. She goes to the desk and takes out a bundle of papers. It contains poems Raja had written during the days of their closeness. For a minute she wants to tear them to bits, empty her desk so that no trace should be left of those heroic days of theirs. She sits shuffling her finger through them. The whole night she sits tearing this paper and that, thus clearing up her papers along with the bitterness she has felt for years. The widening of her mental horizon results in doing away with the bitterness.

Now she is able to visualise everything in the right perspective. At last she realises the inadequacy of her approach to life, and perceives that the true meaning of being can only be achieved through love, not rejection :

> Although it was shadowy dark, Bim could see as well by clear light of day that she felt only love and yearning for them all, and if there were hurts, these gashes and wounds in her side that bled, then it was only because her love was imperfect and did not encompass them thoroughly enough and because it had flaws and inadequacies, and did not extent to all equally. (*CLD* 165).

Thus, at last she realises the narrowness of her approach towards others. The flaw in Bim's love was that of ego-centricity which had prevented her from appreciating, what can be termed, the otherness of others. With the realisation of the inadequacy of her earlier vision of reality as an assertion of will, comes its modification — a quest for the love of others which demands a transcendence of the self. She achieves this spiritual wholeness by consciously choosing to bridge the rift with others which also enables her to find her own social relavance.[30]

When Bim wakes up the next morning she finds her nieces who had arrived early that morning, sitting on her bed waiting for her to wake up, she holds them close to her; she realises that she had not held anyone so close for years. When it is time for Tara to leave, she asks her to give her message to Raja: "Tell him we couldn't come - but he should come. Bring him back with you, Tara -- or tell him to come in winter. All of them... Tell him I'm waiting for him -- I want him to come - I want to see him" (*CLD* 175-76). There is contact, first between Bim and Tara, and then between Bim and Raja. The rift is bridged at last. The house, which had enclosed her as the cocoon encases the larvae, is broken. She emerges a 'new woman' as a butterfly emerges out of the cocoon into the 'clear light of day'.

The foregoing discussion of Anita Desai's novels reveals that all her women protagonists are seekers of a higher meaning from life irrespective of their being within or outside the marital state. They seek self fulfilment through a commitment to a higher ideal and since most of them are married woman, it is quite natural for them to expect their partners in marriage, namely, their husbands to help them realise this ideal.

The 'new women' of Desai's fictive world have their deep commitment to such ideals as spirituality, sharing and companionship based on understanding and sympathy, need for a sensitive approach towards others to understand their emotional and spiritual needs, attempt to understand the others' points of view and the like. But more often than not, they find their male counterparts lacking in commitment to such ideals. The males of Desai's fiction are generally governed by considerations of power and success and as such their views on women's needs, spiritual or worldly, are all dictated by the norms of the male-dominated society. Hence, the absence of a deep commitment to any ideal on the part of their husbands becomes the cause of tension for the women protagonists of Desai. Here it needs to be emphasized that the cause of tension among the women protagonists is not marriage or the institution of marriage and the husband, though the most important part of any marital relationship, just becomes a part of the people around them. From their point of view the husband ceases to be a distinct entity -- he is just an element in the larger set of people around them. This is a new element in their approach. This point becomes quite clear when we analyse how her main women characters view the institution of marriage.

For Maya of *Cry The Peacock* self-fulfilment means recognition of her spiritual and emotional needs. She is not unhappy with her marriage as such. So, in order to bring her husband on her side of commitment, she makes sincere efforts and even makes adjustments but fails and this eventually becomes the cause of her tragedy. It may also be mentioned here that Maya looks for this kind of commitment not only in her husband, Gautama but also among her relatives and present circle of friends. Since all of them are found wanting in it, the husband also becomes just one of the people around Maya. For Nanda Kaul of *Fire on the Mountain* all relationships of her marital state remain at the periphery and because of her deep commitment, she needs no outside help. She carries on with her family people and the husband without being attached. Her commitment to her withdrawal into herself is so deep that she neither confronts nor opposes the people around her. Thus, her commitment becomes her strength. Sita of *Where Shall We Go This Summer?* finds meaninglessness in marriage right from the beginning. This feeling of meaninglessness is so intense that it draws into itself all other relationships issuing from marriage. Even after her 'escape' to the island she realises that she will have to put up with the meaningless relationships of marital life and continue life along with it. The gap between her approach and that of the people around her is unbridgable. But this in no case compels her to give up her basic commitment. Bim in *Clear Light of Day* goes a step further. Towards the end of the novel she comes to realise that the true meaning of being can be realised not only through putting up with others, it lies in the acceptance and appreciation of others' point of view. In passing it may be mentioned that if Bim had married perhaps she would have 'accepted' her husband in the same manner as she accepts her brother Raja and sister Tara.

Thus, for the 'new woman' of Desai's fiction, marriage does not exist as an important issue. They neither seek fulfilment in marriage nor through marriage. At the same time, it is not an assertion of independence by rejecting marriage or viewing marriage as an impediment to self-realisation. Hence, there is no relevance of their attitude to marriage. Marriage has, of course, a dominant place in Desai's novels but it merely becomes the occasion or the instrument to reveal the deeper difference of approach towards the more fundamental and spiritual issues.

The commitment of Desai's women to a full and meaningful life is both deep and conscious. They can recognize the true ring of such life even though they might have only a fleeting glimpse of it. Such is the case with Maya. She sees it in the scene of the husband, wife and the dog and is quick to perceive how all the three— the man, the woman and the animal — share this bond. Maya can also feel the false ring of a life where at the periphery the man and woman are bound together by this bond of love and understanding but this feeling does not reach the core. Such is the case of her Persian lecturer friend, Leila, whose love is not a spiritual urge but a romantic impulse. Sita sees such a vision of selfless love in the image of the old man attending on her dying tubercular wife.

Again, it is this conscious commitment in the women characters which enables them to perceive the moral shallowness of the people around them. Maya realises quite early that her husband is pragmatic, intelligent, patronising but devoid of any commitment. Sita associates dull safe routine with Raman and finds that he can neither travel with her mentally nor emotionally. To Nanda Kaul, the pragmatism of her husband never touches the core of her personality.

These women characters also share a feeling of compassion and tenderness towards everything that is weak and suffering. Maya's love for her pet Toto, her attitude to the bear and the dancing-girls are all illustrative of her basic sympathies which she has for the tender and the weak. Similarly, Sita also experiences feeling of compassion when she sees the eagle being attacked by the crows outside her apartment.

Thus, it becomes clear that the main women characters of Desai's fiction consciously reflect upon and analyse their own feelings and commitments. At the same time, they also analyse the absence of such commitment in the people around them. It is because of the presence of these qualities that the phrase 'the new-women proper' can be applied to the women characters of Anita Desai.

NOTES

1. Anita Desai, "Replies to Questionnaire", *Kakatya Journal of English Studies* 2nd Ser.4 (Aug. 1978): 1.
2. Atma Ram, "An Interview with Anita Desai," *Interviews with Indian English Writers* (Calcutta: Writers Workshop, 1983) 20.
3. Ramesh K. Srivastava, "Anita Desai at Work : An Interview", *Perspectives on Anita Desai,* ed. Ramesh K. Srivastava (Ghaziabad: Vimal Prakashan, 1984) 212.
4. Desai 4.
5. Desai 1.
6. Srivastava 222.
7. Anita Desai, "Women Writers", *Quest* 65 (April/June 1970): 40.
8. Desai, "Women Writers", 41.
9. Ram 32.
10. Srivastava 211.
11. Srivastava 211.
12. Jasbir Jain, *Stairs to the Attic : The Novels of Anita Desai* (Jaipur : Printwell Publishers, 1987) 12.
13. Srivastava 224.
14. Renu Juneja, "Identity and Feminity in Anita Desai's Fiction," *Journal of South Asian Literature 22.1* (Summer, Fall, 1987) : 77.
15. Juneja 77.

16. Juneja 66.
17. Shantha Krishnaswamy, "Anita Desai: The Sexist Nature of Sanity", *The Women in Indian Fiction in English* (New Delhi : Ashish Publishing House, 1984) 240.
18. Anita Desai, *Cry, The Peacock* (New Delhi. Orient Paperbacks, 1990). All subsequent references to this edition will be referred to as *CP*.
19. Anita Desai, *Where Shall We Go This Summer?* (New Delhi : Orient Paperbacks, 1991). All subsequent references to this edition will be referred to as *WSWGTS*.
20. Nimmie Poovaya, "The Emergence of the Feminist Consciousness in Margaret Atwood's *Surfacing* and Anita Desai's *Where Shall We Go This Summer?*," *Commonwealth Litt : Problems of Response* ed. C. D. Narasimhaiah (Bombay : Macmillan India Limited, 1981) 210-211.
21. Shyam Asnani, "New Morality in the Modern Indo-English Novel", *Indian Women Novelists* ed. R. K. Dhawan (New Delhi : Sterling, 1990) 66.
22. Elaine Showalter, *A Literature of Their Own: British Women Novelists from Bronte to Lessing* (Princeton, N. J. : Princeton University Press, 1977) 13.
23. Betty Friedan, *The Second Stage* (New York : Summit Books, 1981) 13.
24. Anita Desai, *Fire on the Mountain* (New York: Penguin Books, 1981). All subsequent references to this edition will be referred to as *FM*.
25. Laxmi Parasuram, "*Fire on the Mountain* : A New Dimension of Feminine Perception", *The Literary Criterion* 16.3 (1981) : 60.
26. Parasuram 61.
27. Ruth K. Rosenwasser, "Voices of Dissent : Heroines in the Novels of Anita Desai", *Journal of South Asian Literature* 24.2 (Summer, Fall, 1984) 102.
28. S. M. Khanna, "Existentialist Overtones in Anita Desai's *Fire On the Mountain*", *Indian Fiction in English : Problems and Promises* ed. R. S. Singh (New Delhi : Barhi Publishers, 1983) 130.
29. Anita Desai, *Clear Light of Day* (London : Penguin Books, 1980). All subsequent references to this edition will be referred to as *CLD*.
30. Jain 129.

5

THE 'ABERRATION' -- I
SHOBHA DE

The two novelists discussed so far belong to the same stream. The development of their women characters is along moral and spiritual lines which means commitment to a system of values, the yearning for a life of fulfilment where fulfilment comes when the woman has a value-system and there is also present an environment in which such values can find expression through sharing and participation. It also means an attempt to view the lot of women in the scheme of things and a heart which understands and sympathises and also goes out to everything that is tender, meek and suffering, including the animals.

In the novels of Kamala Markandaya and Anita Desai, these commitments of the 'new woman' are represented through certain metaphors and images. The questions of economic freedom, social status, security and such things assume a secondary role in the consciousness of the women characters of these two novelists. As regards the process of development of the ideas of commitment, it has already been seen that they first appear in a vague and indistinct form (as in the case of Kamala Markandaya) and later on they become fully established (as in the case of Anita Desai).

However, one might expect the female characters of other women novelists who wrote after these to continue this process of development and grapple with more fundamental problems and aspire towards higher ideals of womanhood. But when we come to Shobha De and Namita Gokhale we find that they have deviated from this stream of development and in their novels the women characters, if at all they could be termed 'new women', represent an entirely different value-system. However, in the process of development of art one often comes across such 'sallies' but they are always brief and art returns to the mainstream of spiritual and moral values. So such 'sallies' which might dazzle for a short spell cannot become a different or a parallel stream which branches off from the mainstream and continues its separate course. Hence, we have called the women characters of Shobha De and Namita Gokhale as 'aberrations'.

The first author in this pattern is Shobha De who began this dazzling 'sally' with her first novel *Socialite Evenings* and continued this through *Starry Nights*, *Sisters* and *Strange Obsession*. Yet a stage came when she also acknowledged the need that the author must return to the mainstream, for after these she came out with *Sultry Days*, about which she says on the title page itself... 'finally a book by me, that they (my children) can read'.

As opposed to the women characters of Kamala Markandaya and Anita Desai, Karuna, the main character and narrator of Shobha De's *Socialite Evenings*[1] is not concerned with the lot of women. But here that concern changes to 'I am the good thing' and even this 'I' does not stand for any commitment to spiritual and moral values but it is 'a good thing' because it can be dressed up and presented as an extremely marketable product over the media. Karuna's pre-occupation with 'I' and 'the good thing is me' becomes clear when the jounalist of a foreign magazine comes up with a proposal to make a documentary with Karuna's experiences as the focal point of such a film. Karuan's reply to such an idea is : "I think it's a great idea. In fact, I think I'll steal it. There may be a documentary in it but I'm going to give a book a shot. I've always wanted to write one-so you can take a walk, Yankeeagent. I know when I'm on to a good thing and the good thing is me. If anyone is going to cash in on this, baby, it is n't going to be you...' (*SE 306*). Since she considers herself the 'good thing', she would not allow anyone else to 'cash in on' her experiences except herself. Thus, every important action or decision of Karuna is governed by the 'I' or 'me' element.

It is not only that she does not reflect on the lot of the women of her own choice but because she is incapable of doing so. Even during the period when she has been divoced by her husband and has to move from place to place in search of a job, her 'being-herself-the-good-thing' kind of attitude does not quite leave her. Her sole concern during this stage, too, is how she can shake off her middle-class background. She is candid enough to own that she abhors the society of women of middle and lower class. She has contempt for their small 'concerns' and their tastes :

> And I hated the poverty, this meagre income forced on me. I suppose I was a bit too old for the drastic changes I had to adjust to or perhaps I just wasn't cut out to be middle class, lower middle class. For a start, there was the matter of transport. I'd never travelled by bus since my school days. Or waited in queues for anything. Getting into a local train and commuting to town was a major trauma. I could not relate to the other women in my compartment. I felt revolted by their small concerns. I'd watch with horror as they squabbled over small change and petty issues. Their conversations depressed me. It was all so much stomach — turing, their talk of vegetable price and milk strckes. Sometimes I'd over-hear a husband being discussed, but it was invariably in servile terms. Every problem of theirs seemed trivial and insignificant to me. The quotidian detail of their lives — spats with the mother-in-law, a child with mumps, school admissions and donation money, husband's stalled promotions, office gossip, a crisis at the nighbourhood creche, an ailing parent, a relative's hernia operation, saree sales at Kala Niketan, haldi verses cold cream, Garden Vareli at a suburban store, discounts at Sahakari Bhandar — *I hated to be in that environment.* Rubber monsoon sandals and drippy raincoats, the musty smell of old saris, BO camouflaged under cheap perfume, the sickening smell of stale-flowers and coconut oil. I didn't belong to this world. I felt nauseated, physically sick. I'd sit there staring at a spot on the partition hoping none of the women would attempt to strike up a conversation with me. I'd watch them devouring cheap novellas as greedily as they dug into their station-bought *Wadapaus*. I'd listen to their comments on the latest exploits of popular film-stars and all the while feel sick at being there, forced into a life style that I'd rejected twenty years ago (*SE* 240-41).

Karuna's lack of sensibility in matters concerning the weak and the suffering such as the animals and the birds and her utter lack of feelings towards these is revealed in the conversation she and her friend

Anjali have about some animals and birds that have been left in the care of Anjali by her 'spiritual mentor' Babaji. Anjali informs Karuna that 'a couple of birds died' after drinking the 'holy water' given by Babaji. To this Karuna's reply is one of casualness and indifference, she merely says, 'May be it was poisoned' (*SE* 203). This is in sharp contrast to the reactions that the death of a pet or the attack on a helpless eagle by the vultures evoke from the heroines of Anita Desai. Even the 'beasts of burden' and the stoned-baby monkey in Kamala Markandaya's *Two Virgins* arouse feelings of compassion for the weak and the suffering in the two sisters. But here no such response is to be seen.

A similar difference in approaches and attitudes is observed when the issue of abortion comes up. The discovery that Karuna is 'pregnant' makes her quite nervous and she is almost in a state of panic. But in this situation, too, her whole response and attitude is directed towards herself. The 'good thing is me' element never allows her to think of the unborn child in the first place. Her initial reaction is:

> What am I supposed to do now? I don't want the bloody baby. I've never wanted one — Krish's or any one else. I don't even know what women are supposed to do when they find themselves knocked up. Should I get myself into a clinic? Which doctor? How do I explain it to the husband? And the mother-in-law —she'll guess like a shot. She's a hawk, always watching me. (*SE* 213)

Later also when she leaves her husband's house and starts living with Anjali, 'the idea of keeping the baby,' does not sink into her system firmly. Once again the consideration is herself — whether her parents would accept her with the child. She gives an inkling of her thoughts after her husband has talked to her at length about the 'settlement':

> For a couple of days after his call I actually toyed with the idea of keeping the baby. May be it was just spite, may be I felt it was what I needed -- someone to call my own as the cliche goes (*SE* 222).

But the moment her friend Anjali hears of such an 'idea' germinating in Karuna's mind, she decides to nip it in the bud. She tells Karuna, 'Don't be crazy ... A baby is a life-long responsibility -- look at me. Are you prepared to tie yourself down for ever? Get a puppy or a kitten if your are feeling all that motherly, forget about a kid. Besides, you won't be able to handle the scene. You are n't cut out for a single parent situation. You can't go around with an orphan Annie-like kid, with no father on the scene' (*SE* 222).

What has been discussed here in a matter-of-fact manner between the two friends is in sharp contrast to the discussion which the two sisters Saroja and Lalitha have in *Two Virgins* after the latter has undergone abortion. A glimpse of their dialogue would reveal how radically different the two approaches are. When Saroja expresses her desire to know the details of the abortion, Lalitha's answer reveals her emotional attachment for the life that was taking shape in the womb :

> They sucked him out, said Lalitha, bit by bit. He came out in pieces. I could feel him going, though they said I would n't feel anything. He would n't have filled a tumbler, except for the fluid. It took ten minutes. She paused, she was hideously dry. If I had n't wanted him it might have been different, an unwanted child is better off unborn. But I did want him. I wanted him most when he was going, these last ten minutes of his life [2]. (*Two Virgins* 232)

The discussion of the two sisters in this case revolves round the human aspect i.e. a life that was being snuffed out and the entire experience of abortion. But what Karuna and Anjali discuss does not contain an iota of concern for the unborn child. The preoccupation seems to be with getting rid of the 'problem' as soon as possible so that Karuna once again becomes 'free' to lead her life the way she wants.

In *Socialite Evenings*, too, there is talk about commitment in life and being in the 'mainstream'. Girish, the great art film maker, exhorts Karuna to take life more seriously and 'commit' herself to some serious thing like cinema :

> 'But life is about more than just goofy kids and surf-boards. I want you to get involved. Commit yourself. Get into the mainstream'. 'The mainstream of what? Cinema? Life? I find all that very complex' (*SE* 255).

What Girish implies is that Karuna should take her role of Shakuntla in his film more seriously. If this is what is meant by 'commitment' and 'mainstream', then it can be easily said that her 'commitment', too, is some kind of an 'aberration'. Even her intellectual pursuits suggest that she is incapable of involving herself in anything serious, for her preoccupation is with only 'cross-word puzzles' and 'newspaper-chess'.

It is quite ironic that Karuna feels repelled by middle-class women 'devouring cheap novellas' in the local train.

Whereas marriage as such is not the concern of the women of Kamala Markandaya and Anita Desai, marriage is a kind of obsession with Karuna and other women in the novel. They hate having a husband, yet they must have one. They want one under the roof, may be as a stranger with whom they could spring up occasional confrontation. Quite early in life Karuna realised that she had been stuck up in a 'meaningless marriage'. With time, to her the husband became a complete stranger and their love-making, too, was some kind of a 'listless affair'. How strange and mechanical their relationship had become can be gauged from the following lines :

> We'd lie in there in the bed-room with the dull walls reading our respective magazines. He with *The Economist* and I with a film rag. If there was absolutely nothing better to do and we ran out of magazines, he'd turn to me and nudge, 'Wife-how about it?' Neither the words nor the tone did anything to allay the disgust I usually felt. But it was simpler to just get on with the damn thing and have it over and done with as fast as possible. I would lie away. Or sometimes I'd mentally review the day's accounts. I can never remember my thought being anything other than unedifying. (*SE* 67)

Women like Karuna and Anjali put up with a stranger-husband not out of choice or any conviction, they need one to afford the luxuries of life. The fact is painfully drummed into Karuna by Anjali when she comes to know that the former has left her husband's house with just one 'Samsonite suitcase' with 'a few essentials in it'. When Karuna tells Anjali that she had not brought anything with her because nothing belonged to her, and that her husband was the rightful owner of everything in the house, Anjali is furious at her. She advises, 'This is not the time for false dignity and pride'... 'Don't be a fool. You are entitled to your things'. She further elaborates her point by saying, '... you need money. I wan n't suggesting you rob the guy. But you are entitled to compensation. You have invested all these many years in marriage — don't you think it's you right to claim something'? If I know that family, they'll cut you off without a dime. That's not fair either. I call that exploitation'(*SE* 217-18).

So, when Karuna's husband comes out with a 'package' deal

containing an assured income and all the luxuries which she had hitherto been enjoying, Karuna's only remark is, '(the package) sounds sweet'. Similar is the case with Anjali. Her second marriage to the homosexual Kumar is nothing but an exchange for 'the Porche, emeralds, holidays in Biarritz, shopping along the Champs-Elysees, a villa in Ooty, parties every night, unlimited Champagne - and the choice to pick my own bed-mate but only discreetly'. The bargain is much more worthwhile than what she would have found in 'a proper married life with a proper husband and a proper home'.

In the kind of social circle to which women like Karuna, Anjali and Ritu belong, a husband is also needed to be shown to everyone as one who has been conquered. Ritu, who is known for her power over men, belongs to this category. She is so much in command that even other women observe about her husband, 'Her husband, well — trained by her, to make the right responses, revelled in her glamour and sex-appeal' (*SE* 108).

Examples of women like Ritu are not common and in most cases the wife has often to demean herself as a woman, as a person and also as a human being but she puts up with it. In the novel we have the example of Anjali who is in full knowledge of the fact that her first husband, Abe seduced all her friends. She once even tells Karuna jokingly, 'I have lost all my girl-friends to Abe. The minute he meets them, he starts his seduction plans. It does n't take very long. One lunch, two drinks — and boom — they're in bed. I don't want to lose you.' The surprising thing is that Anjali never objects and so when she learns that her friend Karuna has refused Abe, she even feels offended!

It is n't that Anjali puts up with Abe's 'seductions' and leaves it at that. When it comes to the scene of her second marriage with Kumar, she even turns a blind eye to Kumar's 'affair' with his homosexual partner, Murty. Even the watching of blue-films by Kumar and Murty does not seem to arouse any sense of revolt on the part of Anjali. She mentions the fact in a very casual manner:

. . . You know K and Murty often watched blue films. It was innocent fun. Whenever they felt bored they' switch on one of these. K used to pick them up at Frankfurt. And he'd bring back a few other sexy-things — again just for fun. We used to laugh at the latest "inventions" and compare them to last year's. Nobody actually used them or anything. In fact, at one party we'd strung up all these fish-tailed condoms and other thingies all over the bar as a joke! But they were all lying there in Murty's room ... (*SE* 208).

The level to which women like Anjali can demean themselves does n't end with putting up with their husband's wayward ways, they even go to the extent of putting up with violence. After Ritu's liaison with Gul, the shady NRI, has run its course, she is made to roganise 'virgins for him and his friends'. In one of the parties when Ritu picks a quarrel with a starlet, Sonia with whom Gul was having a brief 'thing', Gul beats her (Ritu) in public. Anjali describes the indicent to Karuna, '...He also called her some filthy names -- in Hindi. And do you know something? Nobody dared interfere. She just lay there on the ground while he kicked her, yanked her hair, spat on her and tore her blouse' (*SE* 20).

Even the one role that of providing security to the wife which the traditional society has assigned to the husband and against which the so-called emancipated women revolt, even this role is not played by the husband. Kumar chooses to disappear from the scene when his wife Anjali is humiliated in public during the ship party hosted by Varun. The only thing which these emancipated women can do in a fit of boldness is abuse the man in words which even coarse, illiterate women would not use in public. We have only to recall what Karuna tells Karan when she meets him in the Oberoi Hotel and enquires about her friend, Anjali, 'Listen Asshole ... 'Don't give me your fancy lines. You are nothing but cheap male whore. Why don't you leave Ritu alone?' (*SE* 112). Also, Karuna thinks she has become one-up and vindicated herself as a woman by abusing her husband verbally, when he comes with the proposal to remarry her :

> And you waited all this while to tell me. Just get the hell out of my house and life. I don't ever want to see you again. I let you in this time -- but never again. I'll call the cops if you try and invade my home in future. You are even more of a worm than I thought. You deserve Winnie - I hope she's got a wax doll of yours. I'll send her some extra pins to stick into it. Now take your frigging pipe and OUT !!? (*SE* 264).

For the likes of Anjali and Co. marriage also becomes a necessity because it not only provides them security, status and luxuries, but it also enables them to indulge in adultery, for adultery is possible only within marriage. It might begin as a possible escape from a 'meaningless marriage' as happens in the case of Karuna's affair with Krish but once it is discovered she is advised against going on a 'guilt-trip' by Anjali :

> 'Stop feeling martyred', she said sharply and then softened, I'm not making fun of your feelings — please don't think that but what you're saying is not true at all. You are n't an evil person. You have n't harmed anybody - not really. Your infidelity whatever it was and with whosoever is so trivial. Don't blame yourself for it. Even your husband has forgiven you otherwise his attitude would have been different. He would have acted like a real swine and cut you off without a naya paisa. These things can happen to any one ...' (SE 224).

What Anjali says to Karuna is actually a way of scoring an equaliser over the men-folk, for aren't they supposed to forgive them for their infidelities, big or small?

Despite these facets of a woman's personality, *Socialite Evenings* is a success story. Karuna fights her way up after her divorce, gets recognition in advertising and television productions and becomes financially independent. She " -- carves out her own niche in the professionally competitive world of advertising and acquires all the resources to flirt *ad infinitum* which she is shown doing with a married journalist, Ranbir Roy. The novel closes on the same tenor on which it had opened — unlimited freedom to flirt [3] (Chandra 248). That the author also seems to approve of the kind of life Karuna has led becomes clear in the brief third person one paragraph Epilogue wherein she says :

> ... It had been very hard work, this packaging of her life, and often it had almost seemed impossible to finish the book. But now that it was over she felt a certain sadness, autumnal in its intensity ... she loved this time of the day and she willed herself to relax. Tomorrow's anxieties could be dealt with later, today she would rest. (SE 307)

Yet, all said and done, Karuna's success story does not qualify her to be called a 'new woman'. By contrast, even though the heroines of Anita Desai may be failures yet as women they are 'new'

Asha Rani, the heroine of Shobha De's next novel *Starry Nights* is nothing but a continuation of Ritu of *Socialite Evenings*. What Ritu says about herself regarding her relationship with men also holds good in the case of Asha Rani. Like Ritu, Asha Rani, too, seems to be saying, "All the men I've ever known have always fallen in love with me" (*SE* 107). But unlike Ritu, her power over men is n't just 'fun'. She knows its 'uses' too well to use them to her advantages.

Starry Nights [4] again is a story wherein the so called modern and emancipated women remain obsessed with men. They are all the time engaged in observing men and their ways. This enables them to calculate to what extent men are to be cultivated and when it is the right time to drop them. How far can they be manipulated to suit their ends? All this does not leave any time for these women to think about their own lot or address themselves to more fundamental questions. In other words, they, in no way approximate to the 'new women' of our study. Their total absorption with men does not leave any scope for involvement. In fact, their total absorption with men leads to their obsession with them. And since they lack involvement and commitment to any higher ideal, these women, too, are 'aberrations'. Asha Rani represents this 'aberration'.

For Asha Rani the road to stardom has meant manipulating many a man right from the level of Assistant Producer to important underworld dons and industrialists. In the beginning of the novel we hear Asha Rani telling Kishen Bhai, "All of you are just the same, but wait, I will show you, I will do to men what they try to do to me. I will screw you all -- beat you at your own game" (*SN* 8). Thus, 'beating men at their own game' is the strategy that Asha Rani resorts to throughout the novel.

With her arrival in the world of Bollywood, her 'game' takes off with no signs of letting up till the end. The first 'contact' she and her mother find worth cultivating in Bombay is Kishenbhai, a small producer of little consequence. He is the one who gives Asha Rani the first required 'break' in the film industry but not without extracting the cost from her body. He is the first one to 'de-flower' Asha Rani. But once Asha Rani has acquired the status of a heroine, she is in no mood to continue as 'baby Jaan' to Kishenbhai. The moment Asha Rani's 'affections' are directed towards Akshay Arora, the reigning stud of 70 mm, Kishenbhai tries to discourage her from getting involved with the latter. At this juncture, Kishenbhai becomes a pathetic figure. He himself admits :

> But who was he to moralize? He was not her father, or her brother. He was just an ex-lover. In the film-industry, nothing was as worthless as a discarded paramour. Especially one who was a professional has-been. What would he have told her? Don't sleep with that —? She would have replied, 'Did n't you too sleep with me? Where were your scruples then? You also had a wife. And children. You used me. You exploited me. So how are you any different from Akshay? And she would have been right. Except that there was one important difference. Somewhere down the line Kishenbhai had made a *bewakoof* of himself. He had fallen in love with Asha Rani (*SN* 8).

Asha Rani and her Amma are quick to realise that it is Shethji, the politician and underworld don who is capable of pulling the strings in the film industry. His favours can turn Asha Rani from a simple heroine to a 'star'. The opportunity presents itself after her brief showdown with Akshay. On receiving 'summons' from Sheth Amirchand's office, Asha Rani 'prepares' herself to meet her benefactor :

> This time Asha Rani had decided against a sari. She wanted to look youthful and different. The Salwar-Kameez she chose was a flattering one with a snug bodice that showed curves to advantage. She wore heels. Some men liked them, some did n't, she calculated that the Shethji would get impressed since he was n't very tall himself... On an impulse, she grabbed a stick of disco-dust and rubbed some spangles between her breasts ... Perfect. She could take on the Shethji ... and half-a-dozen others. (*SN* 59)

After her 'meeting' with the Shethji, Asha Rani very shrewdly refuses the sum offered to her. She is quite confident that she would 'recover it from the Shethji twenty times over'. Asha Rani's gamble pays off immediately. Amirchand is so pleased with her 'performance' that he decides to do something about her non-existent career. A few strategic pulls of the strings from Shethji's end help Asha Rani bag the lead role in the biggest-producer Neteshji's latest extravaganza. The title song of the film — 'Love, Love, Kiss, Kiss, — turns out to be the biggest 'hit song of the decade' and Asha Rani's career swings into the fastest track in filmdom. Plus, the Shethji becomes her eternal mentor to closely take care of her rise and fall in the industry.

THE 'ABERRATION' - I

Not content with her success in the commercial cinema, Asha Rani tries to make her entry into thhe world of art cinema also.

The director of the art film, Suhas is hard to please. But Asha Rani 'uses' the occasion of outdoor shootings to her fullest advantage. Asha Rani evokes the 'interest' of the otherwise out-and-out professional man Suhas by deciding to 'celebrate' his birthday in a very special way. A drunken Suhas lurches towards Asha Rani's 'naked body' but she tries to extricate it from his clumsy embrace and say, 'No, we'll do it my way today. I want you to remember this birthday forever' (SN 86). Since Suhas is not easily aroused, Asha Rani has a different way of handling such men: "Experience told her that Suhas's seduction was going to pose problems. Expertly, she used her tongue, lips, fingers and teeth to arouse the man who lay passively beside her" (SN 86). The 'expert handling' yields rich dividends. Asha Rani's earthy 'new look' publicity stills are to be found not only on just the popular film magazines but they also figure on the covers of some more serious magazines along with quite a few write ups. The awards also follow in turn. Hence, in less than seven years, Asha Rani is able to crack the commercial film jackpot.

If people like Kishenbhai, Amirchand and Suhas have proved beneficial to Asha Rani in her professional life, the likes of Akshay Arora, Amar and Abhijit carry on with their 'entries' and 'exits' in the personal life of Asha Rani. She gets involved with Amar only to show Akshay that 'she could get a new lover — a much younger one'. Amar, in turn, uses her as a springboard to stardom. Abhijit Mehra, the son of an industrialist, is also 'used' as a stop-gap arrangement during the period when she is off Akshay.

Asha Rani's short -- lived affair with Abhijit lands her in New Zealand where she meets Jay whom she marries and starts leading a comfortable life. She lives in this state for five long years with her family in an alien country. It is n't that she loves jay or has some real feelings for him. 'Jay had been an out for her, an escape route' (*SN 191*). But for all that Jay does for Asha Rani, she feels indebted. She even admits that Jay provided him the status of a wife which in her circumstances would not have been possible in India :

> And I too had lost my head, become, a loose woman. You never questioned me about my past. You did n't question me about the other men, other affairs. You helped me to put my life back

together again. You showed me that another, better life was possible for a woman like me. In India, no man, that is no decent man, would have married me, given me his name, looked after me the way you have done. If I had found a husband, it would have been some scoundrel after my money, or marrying me for fame. Most probably I would have ended up like Amma. May be Amirchand would have kept me. Or another Abhijit would have come my way (*SN* 169).

This self-analysis and this remorse is, however, short-lived and back home, her 'fidelity' runs its course and she is once again busy 'using' Jojo for bagging a suitable role to mark her re-entry into the film world.

Thus, what Asha Rani does with her life gives her a lot of money and fame but her scheming and manipulation leave her with little time for commiting herself to anything deeper and higher. The near-absence of any commitment on her part renders her character what we call an 'aberration'.

The fifth novel of Shobha De, *Sultry Days* [5] does contain women who are obsessed with men; they, too, indulge in beating men at their own game but here we also come across some glimpses of commitment thereby giving credence to the fact that not all writings of Shobha De are 'aberrations' and that there is a possibility of even her returning to the mainsteam of writing after a few 'sallies'.

Unlike the other two novels discussed so far, *Sultry Days* [5] has apparently a man as the central character. The narrator of the protagonist is, however, a woman but it is through the male character Deb that Nisha discovers herself. From the beginning we become aware of Nisha's attraction for Deb who is also referred to as God by most of his college Chums. She is attracted to Deb because he is a mixture of opposites. His appearance is shabby, wears days' old stubble, always scratches his 'matted locks which were full of licenests', smokes 'beedies', is a man of loose morals, 'has had several girls by the time he reached college'. His attitude towards girls is also simple — 'use them and leave them'.

Despite his shabby appearance, 'God's hands and fingernails were surprisingly, neat and clean'. He knows many languages such as German, French and Spanish. He had already read Chaucer and Karl Marx before leaving school. He is the son of a communist and himself a communist, gets arrested while taking out morchas. He even got a scholarship in Columbia University but since 'comrade' could n't pay the air-fare he could n't make it. On the finer side, he is a lover of classical music, himself plays the flute extremely well and knows all the Beetles songs by heart. With all these qualities on his side God is also a chronic hanger-on but it is the visionary and the rebel in him that attracts Nisha towards him. About why she has chosen God as her boy friend out of all the other 'guys' Nisha says : 'I didn't want to go for other guys, damn it. God was all I wanted — had ever wanted in a boy-friend. He was n't like the other boys. He had character - you know? It came out at different moments. Like the time he stood up to Rakesh whose sole claim to fame was being the only son of a sugar baron' (*SD* 8).

God's entry into the 'literary circuit' is through proof-checking but he soon discovers that he can do more than just read other people's proofs. With his association with Art Magazine *Plume*, God's career takes an upward turn. It is actually the beginning of the death of the rebel and the visionary in him. As *Plume* progressed, God, too, 'changed more than he cared to admit'. He no longer played the flute, even stopped talking to his motorbike 'Bijli'. He is busy 'cultivating' those very people he once detested. A quick look at his changed routine would reveal what a changed man God is after his alignment with the capitalist circuit :

> It was true that God had changed more than he cared to admit. He was out at some five star clip joint or the other night after night. Often, he'd begin his day with a breakfast-meeting at the Shamiana, with a quick lunch at China-garden, a cocktail party in an opulent setting and if he had room for dinner after stuffing himself with chicken tikkas and shami kababs, then a bite at an all-night coffee- shop (with beer) before going home to his shabby chawl (*SD* 99).

Nisha, who has closely known God since his college days finds all this very disturbing and difficult to understand. According to her, 'God was selling out'.

Thus, God starts sinking in the estimate of Nisha. To her God had at one time symbolised 'commitment' but gradually he loses all shreds of self-respect. As for Nisha, hers is a very ordinary course of life wherein she tries to make her mark through sheer hard work and application. Although herself a member, yet she always remains at the periphery of affluent and glamorous life. In other words, she is quite unlike the other women of Shobha De who revel in the life of glamour and sex. Here it may be remarked that it is the 'commitments' of God that help Nisha to remain at the periphery of such a life.

As God gets more and more the taste of 'power' and 'money', his commitments appear to be psuedo-commitments. Although Nisha does not have any pronounced commitments of her own yet her constant companionship with Deb reveals the gulf between herself and Deb's psuedo-commitments. That she does not approve of God's 'new' way of life is made clear several times by her in the course of the narrative. One such reaction would suffice here :

> No I did n't like what was happening to God at all. We were beginning to see less and less of each other now that he did n't need to touch me for cash that often. He was getting ahead professionally, meeting all the VIPs in town, inter viewing culture vullures and generally being wooed by 'all those who mattered' in the high-life of the city. (*SD* 100)

Even the occasional meeting between Nisha and God turns out to be a confrontation. After one such 'meeting' God calls her 'Jhooti bitch' and Nisha's rejoinder is 'Capitalist Kutta'. This is the nadir of their relationship. It is actually the point when Nisha has completely seen through his so-called 'commitments'.

And simply by not becoming a part of God's psuedo-commitments, Nisha begins to discover her own commitments. Her commitment towards the end of the novel emerges as a commitment to a cause. She exposes Yashwantbhai through her write ups and remains undeterred despite God's warnings 'to keep herself off by having anything to do with Yashwantbhai and his under-world connections'. She is joined in her 'cause' by her mother and her activist friend Pratimaben. Nisha's mother and Pratimaben are out to expose Yashwantbhai on the issue of his 'atrocities' on Pramila with whom Yashwantbhai had an illicit relationship for some time.

Thus, we see that by dedicating herself to a 'cause' the character of Nisha rises. Actually Nisha's rise has to be seen in the context of the degeneration of God's character. It is only when Nisha has some inkling of her 'commitments' that she is able to seek some kind of an identification with the women and men--folk of the middle class. Her attitude towards them is very different from that of Karuna of *Socialite Evenings*. There the guiding motto for Karuna is 'I am the good thing' but here this 'I' and 'me' get transformed into 'We' and 'they'. This is a great development and when such a transformation has taken place there is no element for hatred-- it just turns into a fellow-feeling for others. Nisha gives evidence of such feelings while she is rushing to the hospital to see wounded Deb. Her identification with the people of lower and middle class is almost complete:

> It had n't registered at all. I did n't even want to know the details. Instead, I concentrated on the dabba wallahs charging out of the railway station and hurtling down the street, bearing home-cooked lunches for thousands of down-town office-goers. All sorts of pictures lashed through my mind: I thought of the wives who woke up at five a.m. to start cooking for their husbands so that lunch would be ready by 8.30... And I wondered what sort of lives these couples led. Did they communicate or merely talked. Did they have intense relationships or just matter-of-fact ones? Did they relate to one another or did they merely tolerate their mates? Did their children get their share of 'quality time' or did they have to make do with whatever scraps that came their way? ....
>
> I *envied* these women their uncomplicated lives. All they had to bother about was getting the dabba ready on time for the dabbawallah. Nobody of theirs ever got shot. Nobody threatened them through the mail or over the phone, they did not have to ferret out interesting little nuggets about people in order to write hot copy ... (*SD* 219-20)

Another quality which helps Nisha to rise in our estimate is her capacity to distance herself and view herself objectively even at the most traumatic moments. Her 'encounter' with Iqbal, the painter is the best example. Even during the moment when he is about to rape her she can distance herself and pass a judgement on her folly:

> 'You asked for it. Don't say you did n't. You knew when you climbed those stairs with him and entered this place exactly what was in store for you. Don't blame him. Blame yourself, you little fool' (*SD* 158)

It is also a comment on where the so-called emancipated woman might land herself in. The same capacity to distance herself enables Nisha to portray the abortive rape-attempt as something revolting and anti-climatic :

> Now he'd pushed me down after kicking his cans of paint to one side. He climbed on to my rigid body, animal grunts escaping from his wide open mouth. I could see the cavities in his teeth... He looked revolting. I felt his fingers trying to enter me. Just his paint covered fingers. Nothing else. I wanted to laugh. I visualized what the insides of my legs would look like later with streaks of green, blue, vermilion, I waited... expecting something else to happen. It didn't. Iqbal, the great womanizer was limp. He looked pathetic at that moment with his jaw open and eyes shut in psuedo-orgasmic bliss. Gently I pushed him away and fixed my clothes. I looked at Iqbal's famous nudes. There was nothing even remotely erotic about them any more. (*SD* 158)

It is n't that Nisha's distancing and objectivity remains confined to her own actions. During the course of the narrative certain other characters, especially those of educated, modern, emancipated women, are also mentioned. Although they in no way form part of the main story, yet whenever they find their reference, the narrator does not approve of their morals and their life style. The description of the women in the 'new women' category with MBA degrees, wearing business suits and insisting on being addressed as Ms and with whom workaholism has become a fashionable word does not get the approval of the narrator. The lives of such women, in the eyes of the narrator, lack-depth and a sense of purpose and hence are not worth emulating.

But there is another category, that of single women whose description by the narrator is of considerable significance. Such women complain of a 'void' in their lives. It is an emotional and spiritual void that they talk about. Unlike their married counterparts they don't choose to hide it. They may not verbalize it but they betray consciousness of it. The comment of one such woman reveals the consciousness of this kind of void :

> She'd put her finger on it neatly ... We lived with that one hope — that we'd be saved by some man. Most of us hated to admit this, but it was true. Being single was n't such a hot alternative, though many of our married friends thought so. But even those women could sense our desperation, our loneliness,

and feel smug that they had husbands to call their own. They were Mrs. so-and-so. (*SD* 211)

It is quite significant to note that towards the end of the novel Karuna of *Socialite Evenings* decides to spend the rest of her life as a single person but she gives no evidence of the consciousness of any such 'void' in her life.

The narrator also exposes the hollowness and the superficialities of the so-called modern women and their families. Among many examples cited in the novel that of the Baroohas deserves special mention. Nothing can be more shocking than the description of the Baroohas with their children :

> The baroohas had one anthem — 'Our children terrify us' which they did. Their son was nineteen, their daughter seventeen and between them they had succeeded in terrorizing their parents to a point where they were actually frightened to being in the same room with their offspring. Servants reported with glee that often Vikki-baba threw assorted *objets* at his mother and called her names ranging from 'nympho' to 'bitch'. The daughter, Sweeti, adopted different tactics — she killed her parents with cruelty. Cold-blooded mental cruelty. It was a constant refrain, an unending taunt, 'where were you when I got my first period? Where were you when they threw me out at school? Where were you when I met with an accident? Where were you when my boy-friend knocked me up and I nearly bled to death on some quack's operating-table? ...' *(SD* 168)

The Baroohas feel terrified of their children not because of what has happened to their children, they are terrified because they do not wish to confront or introspect the shallowness of the kinds of lives they lead. The children actually act as mirrors wherein they can see their own images and the superficialities of their existence. What they have been avoiding so far, their children force them to confront.

In the novel there is one woman character whose experience sums up in a nutshell the course charted by women characters whom we have called 'aberrations'. It also shows that the only ray of hope for such women is to return to their roots and join the mainstream. This woman character is Pramila.

Pramila is a Nagpur woman who had every thing that a traditional woman could ask for — "a husband with a 'solid' job, security, lovely children, a moped of her own and all the time in the world to pursue her interests" (*SD* 160), yet she felt bored, suffocated and frustrated in this environment. She had talent. This put ideas in her head and she set on the road of becoming an emancipated woman. She started writing poems and within a year she decided that Nagpur was not the place for her and her talents. Suddenly, without informing anyone she went to Bombay. There her poems were translated into English and she moved from success to success.

In order to become 'the completely emancipated woman' she divorced her husband and took her two daughters with her. These, then were the stages in the path of her becoming the emancipated woman : boredom and frustration with her surroundings — disappearing from Nagpur and appearing on the Bombay scene, taking up English writing and discarding Marathi and divorcing her husband. In this world of glamour a stage comes when she overreaches herself. She miscalulates that Yashwantbhai, an underworld king and mafia don is in her power. This results in a traumatic experience wherein her life is threatened and she is forced to go in hiding

After the traumatic experience she is for some time a shattered woman but when Nisha's mother and Partimaben find her out and take up her cause against Yashwantbhai, she discovers a new meaning in life. She fearlessly exposes Yashwantbhai. Though she does not succeed in making any impression upon Yashwantbhai and though she knows that Yashwantbhai's present inaction does not mean that he has accepted defeat and that he is coolly waiting for the time when he can strike back, yet Pramila has found a cause. The cause is to join the movement which seeks to expose persons like Yashwantbhai. This changes her life and she returns to the roots where she belongs. The narrator describes her 'return' in the following way :

> ... She was back with her old Maharashtrian publishing cronies. Back to the people she had arrogantly rejected before moving on to the glamorous world of English language journalism. Shruti (her daughter) was going to a neighbourhood Marathi medium school and Pramila was busy putting together a collection of Marathi poems in tortured metre. (*SD* 224)

NOTES

1. Shobha De, *Socialite Evenings* (New Delhi : Penguin Books, 1989). All subsequent references to this edition will be referred to as *SE*.

2. Kamala Markandaya, *Two Virgins* (New Delhi : Bell Books, 1977) 232.

3. Subhash Chandra, "Family and Marriage in Shobha De's *Socialite Evenings*", *Indian-Women Novelists*, ed. R. K. Dhawan (New Delhi: Sterling Publishers, 1990) 248.

4. Shobha De, *Starry Nights* (New Delhi : Penguin Books, 1991). All subsequent references to this edition will be referred to as *SN*.

5. Shobha De, *Sultry Days* (New Delhi : Penguin Books, 1994). All subsequent references to this edition will be referred to as *SD*.

6

THE 'ABERRATION' – II
NAMITA GOKHALE

One does not comes across examples of such 'aberration' only in high-class societies as is depicted in the novels of Shobha De. 'Aberration' is not confined to the self-conscious, emancipated and educated woman. The 'new woman' of this study is a woman who has commitments, spiritual values and she seeks fulfilment in these terms. And since one can come across such a woman in any social environment, it follows that the woman who represents an 'aberration' can also exist in any class of society. Shobha De's novels portary a highly urbanised and affluent metropolitan society. So her women characters belong to that society. When we turn from Shobha De to Namita Gokhale we find such characters in upper-middle class society and also in a metropolitan-slum.

The first novel of Namita Gokhale, *Paro: Dreams of Passion*[1] centres around the lives of two women characters, Paro and Priya. Both these women make an attempt to shake off the shackles of social convention. But it is only Paro who actually unloosens herself from the shackles. For, in this process a woman has first to liberate herself from her middle-class pseudo-morality in order to break herself free from male-dominance. Though Priya also tries to liberate herself from her middle — class mental and moral make — up, she cannot reach the same level of 'emancipation' as Paro does. Both the women use the same technique — manipulating the opposite sex to achieve their ends. Occasionally, both of them try to look for some kind of meaning from life but since they lack commitment to any ideal or vision, they cannot find such a meaning.

Quite early in the novel, Priya, who is also the narrator of Paro's story and her own, informs us how unconventional and modern Paro made her appearance at her own wedding — reception. When she marries B.R., the sewing machine industrialist, the whole scene is shocking to middle — class sensibility of Priya and even to Paro's parents :

> Her audacity and confidence took my breath away. This was not how brides behaved in my world. All the brides I had ever encountered kept their sari pallus convered, and their heads so perilously downcast as to appear anatomically endangered. But she stood proud and straight, and led the way, with B. R. and her parents trailing after her. Her father, I knew, was a Brigadier (Retd.), and her mother too looked an average member of the upper middle class. Both had polite vacant smiles fixed uneasily to their faces, and they appeared in every way too mundane and ordinary to have bred so exotic a creature as the shimmering bride before them.
>
> She circulated through the room with an assured catlike grace. One inclined hand carelessly held on to, horror of horrors, a glass of gin. The other was graciously bestowed on B.R., who followed in her wake, a slightly glazed look in his fine eyes. (*Paro* 14)

For an 'emancipated' being like Paro, mariage is something which cannot be treated as something permanent. In one of the conversations with Priya she gives her views about 'marriage' in one brief sentence : 'I always knew it (marriage) sounded too good to last'. And it did n't? After her brief marital stint with B.R., Paro starts 'living in open adulterous sin' with 'Bucky Bhandpur, test cricketer and scion of a princely family'. And when Priya asks her about B. R., in her 'quite unconcerned way' she replies, 'He used to be my husband' (*Paro* 27).

Not content with having divorced a husband and having lived with a lover in open adultery, the next target of Paro's sexual journey is Airnendra whom Priya calls 'Lenin' on account of his leftist leanings and outfit. For Avinendra, Paro is a mother-cum-lover figure. In between, Paro also acts as the mistress of Shambhu Nath Mishra, an unscrupulous Minister. Her last and final sexual adventure is her marriage to the Greek film-maker, Loukas Leoros, who is a professed homosexual.

Priya, who has closely watched the sexual journey of Paro, feels that Paro's adventures have liberated her 'from marriage and convention'. Despite her age, she still has the zest for living and is in no mood to call it a day. We have only to remind ourselves of the comment Priya makes about Paro at this juncture :

> This is the Paro who is but recently liberated from marriage and convention: she is still convinced that she is as young and desirable as she was. Her massive breasts, like the enlarged pores of her skin, have grown ponderous with age. Even her fingers have become fatter - but this coarsening of body has also somehow catalysed a startling vitality of mind, a vigour that is as crude as it is real. Life has not tired her — she is undiminished, she has grown. She is still obsessed, loudly and clamorously, with questions that the rest of us answered, or decided not to answer, at some period around adolesence. (*Paro* 26)

What Priya feels for Paro is also echoed by Avinendra (Lenin). For him Paro is 'the free woman, symbol and prototype of emancipation'. His knowledge of the facts that Paro has left a husband and a lover and has a small son of ambiguous parentage do not in any way change his opinion on her. In one of the gatherings of the social elite, he says about Paro, "Now this lady ... is a real individual. She has the courage of her convictions. She is not a kept woman ; she is free. That is why I love her" (*Paro* 43).

It is quite relevant to understand how Paro is able to manipulate so many males in her life and all this in open defiance of the norms of male-made social order. Priya, too, feels perturbed by such a question. To her straight question : "how it was that she managed to manipulate people the way she did', Paro's outright answer is, "It's part of being a beautiful woman. It's a full-time occupation. And much harder work than it seems. But it has its rewards, I confess" (*Paro* 54).

How the man-made laws of the society of which she is a part are to be exploited she is fully aware. When Priya questions Paro regarding 'using' B. R.'s money after their divorce, her curt reply is, 'They made the rules.' In other words, what she wishes to suggest is that when a woman chooses to be defiant, she can beat man at his own game. Another example wherein we find Paro getting even with men is the game of sexual flirtation. Soon after her marriage to B.R., she once discovers B.R. 'screwing' their neighbour's daughter. This horrifies Paro beyond her tolerable limits and she makes a suicide bid by wounding herself with a knife.

But this evokes no reaction in B.R. This is the moment when Paro takes a momentous decision : "After that, I decided I would pay him back in his own coin. I mean — every one was in love with me, and who do you think could ever love that guy?" And Paro embarks on her mission 'to pay (man) back in his own coin'. The result is her sexual adventure spree. It is no wonder then that the likes of Lenins and Shambhu Nath Mishras remain under eternal bondage to her.

But in the midst of all this sexual activity, there are also some moments when Paro asks herself where this kind of life has landed her in. In an honest confession she tells Priya, "Oh, I'm doing it (theatre-going) in an attempt to know myself. I mean, I've spent the last umpteen years fucking the men in my life, and getting fucked myself in the process" (*Paro* 90). She makes this confession when she comes to inform Priya that she has of late taken to play-acting. She further adds that Lenin's marriage has sparked off a desire in her to know herself and as if for a change, she tells Priya, 'And if there is one thing I'm certainly not on to these days ... it's men. That's one scene I don't need, thank you very much.' This desire to 'know' herself takes her to theatre-acting. She gets a role to play Clytemnestra in *Aeschylus*. For her this amounts to having 'something to pour one's energies into.' But this 'play-acting' is short-lived and Paro is next heard of when she accompanies Shambhu Nath Mishra on a foreign tour. Immediately after this her marriage with Loukas Leoros is reported. Thus, Paro's flirtation with art is as momentary as her 'one-night stands.'

Paro who has successfully handled all her amorous adventures, is quick to realise that without her beauty and physical charm she would no longer continue to have her sway over men. Towards the end of the novel, Paro throws a party to celebrate her recovery after the 'accident'. The realisation that her 'charm' is no longer on her side forces her to slash her wrists and put an end to this meaningless sex adventure spree.

The shortest and the easiest way for Paro to rise above her middle class background is through exploiting her own sexuality. The knowledge that her body is something which she can put to use comes to Paro as a teenage girl. This experience has another side to it. Paro's family is horrified and feels a sense of shame when they come to know of it. But to Paro it comes as a triumph over her family. This is something like an immature and middle class version of Karuna's (of *Socialite Evenings*) declaration 'I am the good thing.' Karuna is mature and clever enough to turn her experience into a successful item for the media. Paro uses her sexuality to achieve success in life but basically there is not much difference between the two women. Neither of them looks beyond herself.

Once inhibitions and moral barriers cease to exist, then the society lady, Paro is in quest of sexual variety. "As she is narcissistic, she is unable to discern that sex is no substitute for happiness, that sexual indulgence is coarsening and devitalizing rather than revitalizing"[2] (Bharucha 67). At this juncture, her sexual exploits are the expressions of "the free woman, symbol and prototype of emancipation and individuality" (*Paro* 48) — a person dependent on nobody — being her "own person".

Thus, a search to establish one's sexuality is identical with a search for creativity, to do something new. When crevity in Art is not possible, "Paro seeks an expression of creativity through sexual licence-creativity herein being the charting out of her own definition of dilettantish course of life"[3]. (Bharucha 68). Conversely, for the man and business tycoon B.R., "sex indulgence" is an escape from the reality of "thought, emotion and feeling" (*Paro* 40), and a warning to married men to fulfil their wives' carnal desires, and so prevent any sexual pieca dilloes on their part. In this respect sex for B. R. was a "duty, a vocation, a calling" (*Paro* 40) whereby he reached out to the world and acted as "a lamp-post, or a letter-box for women to send messages to their husbands." Thus, affluence and sexual promiscuity go hand in hand, and a member of affluent society experiences neither guilt nor remorse, for permissiveness is the norm of conduct in such a society.

If *Paro* represents the fact of sexual indulgence amongst the jet-set, or the highly westernised urban Indian, the novel can also be regarded as a working class girl's ambition to liberate herself from the tardy, shoddy and tedious middle class suburban existence. It is of little consequence if this necessitates compromising herself in order to win her employer's approval, for, it could also be a means to gratify her own animal instincts. Priya, who narrates the story has something of a fascination for Paro. She writes about Paro and B. R. because she sees herself in Paro. The fact that Paro snatches away B.R. with whom Priya herself has had a sexual liaison, is a hurt that Priya can 'neither forget nor forgive'. 'This book, too, is a vindication', she says. Yet, proportionate to her hatred for Paro is her own lesbian attraction for her, and, above all, a voyeuristic participation in all the activities of Paro :

Gradually, she became an obsession for me. Subconsciously I would find myself mouthing her words ... I too would throw back my head in a deep throaty laugh, and my eyes would narrow in a pale shadow of her piercing gaze. I would lie under the blue floral Bombay Dyeing coverlets, and dream about them ... I could picture him (B.R.) slowly undressing her; my breath would quicken as he held each firm white breast in his long brutal fingers; I could see the glazed look in his eyes as he sat astride her. Somewhere, our roles would be transposed and I would become her, and feel a triumphant power in his climax, and arrive myself at heaven's gates, to the feverish clutch of my index finger. (*Paro* 16-17)

Paro represents the dreams of passion and social glitter and emancipation that Priya can never realise. Yet within the humble surroundings of her middle-class existence, Priya does make efforts to 'emancipate' herself socially and morally. How much dissatisfied Priya is with her murky household in Andheri can be discerned from her own observation about her situation : "I would awake disoriented in our small all-purpose hall-cum-dining-room, suffused with shame and contempt for the poverty and meanness around me. I would vow to rise from that mire : I would dream of grace, of beauty and harmony" ... (*Paro* 17).

But she is conscious of the fact that her asthmatic mother and a phlegmatic brother can only hinder her dreaming. So she decides to crystallise her 'dreams of passion' into a steady ambition, namely, to capture a husband with status. Like Paro, Priya, too, realises quite early in life that men are to be used for women's personal situations. Hence, when she is shown the photograph of Suresh, 'an owlish youth leaning on a Standard Herald Car', her calculative impulses start working and she gives her consent to marry him. Here, she is forthright in declaring that 'the car decided me'.

In the strata of society to which Priya belongs, for an unmarried girl morality is synonymous with virginity and all brides are supposed to present their virginity as a wedding gift to their husbands. But in Priya's case she had lost her virginity before her marriage. This fact did not give rise to any apprehension in her that her husband might find it out. In her own words she comments how she has been able to turn the value-system of male-dominated society upside down. "My marriage was middle-class one, much as any other. My husband was a virgin, and did not seem to notice that I was not. B. R. accepted my resignation with equanimity ... Suresh unburdened his ambitions, his hopes and dreams to me. He wanted to prove himself to make it" (*Paro* 22).

During the early part of her married life with Suresh, Priya's attempts to become a society lady are not encouraged by Suresh. He tolerates her going to the beauty parlour 'to get her hair set' but he resists her taking to smoking and even tries to restrain her from wearing anything but saris. For a while Priya retreats 'into her Indian wife image' but only to rise again with another card up her sleeve. This time it is again Suresh whom she uses as a tool for her personal ends ; she is honest enough to confess : "I realised that my only weapon in an indifferent world was Suresh and I decided to groom him patiently until my ministrations bore dividends" (*Paro* 34).

Priya's grooming of Suresh does pay dividends and both the husband and the wife embark on an 'assiduous and intensive programme of cultivation'. Soon they also become a part of the elite where it is not camaraderie that binds its members together but 'an intense competitiveness'.

Again, in the kind of society Priya aspires to belong to 'one-man - for-one-woman' norm does not seem to exist. Here extra-marital affairs and casual 'flings' are not things which are considered extra oridnary. In the circumstances, it is quite natural for Priya also to enter into a similar relationship. The opportunity comes when she visits Bombay and meets her ex-boss, B.R. The earlier liaison is again established and Paro seems to be enjoying every moment of it without any tinge of guilt. Priya's description of her second brief stint with B.R. explains her ecstatic state :

I would meet B. R. almost every evening and have dinner with him, with wine, candlelight, roses and all the trappings of a covert ramance. We would make love in anonymous hotel rooms. I would punctuate his appointments and draft short memos of passion in his absences. We would copulate with a love that was both urgent and tender, he would examine every pore and crevice of my body with the wonder of a treasure that has been washed back from the sea ...

It was a second youth, a middle-aged revival of dreams. I had indeed never even dreamt of such passion, and I kept delaying the inevitable return to Delhi and Suresh's clumsy hateful arms ...

Bombay held me in thrall. Those were the happiest days of my life. (*Paro* 36-37).

But like everything 'adultery (also) ran its course and Priya soon returns to Delhi. At home Suresh very hesitatingly tells Priya that during her absence he had heard some 'gossip' about her and B.R. He even goes to the extent of reassuring her that he trusts her fully but feels that 'it is not good for women from good families to be talked about.' Priya, who is confident of manipulating Suresh the way she likes, refuses point blank of any such relationship between her and B. R. Thus, Priya is able to get a 'reprieve' from her otherwise gullible husband.

Even towards the end of the novel when Suresh finds out about the relationship of his wife and B. R. through Priya's diary, Priya does not feel repentant at all. She minces no words in declaring that what she has written about B. R. and herself is fully true and not a figment of her imagination. As for Suresh, she is equally honest in telling him that she never had any real sentiment for him :

> 'And if you think', I said, turning my attention to Suresh, 'if you think I ever had, or could have had, any sentiment except ... no, not hatred, you're not even worth of that ... if you think I could have any sentiment for you except ridicule — then you are an egotistical fool; I've lived with you like a whore, because you paid for it? (*Paro* 102).

The resultant separation between Priya and Suresh also does not make Priya repentant for what she had done. And Priya's 'acceptance' by her husband does not amount to any magnanimity on his part. The fact that Suresh tells Priya that they can give their marriage another trial is suggestive of Suresh's acceptance of her in a manner an estranged husband would return to his wife and home with no feelings of guilt attached.

What Priya does in her marital life qualifies her to be called an emancipated modern woman who has shed some of the inhibitions imposed on a woman in the male-made social order. But even during her experience as an emancipated being, she too, like Paro, feels the urge to look for something deeper, something higher than what she has been able to achieve through the gratification of her senses. After her 'miscarriage', in order to escape the ennui and the boredom she takes to 'reading' while working in a book-shop. But since this is not linked to the core of her personality, it remains only a time-killing hobby and is soon abandoned.

So far under the category 'aberration' the study has dealt with either upper-class women of highly urbanised society (Shobha De's characters) or middle-class women who aspire to rise above their middle-class background. They are not women with commitment to a value-system. If at all they have any commitment, they have it to themselves. Yet they have some sort of dissatisfaction with the society and its laws which have been made by man.

But there is another dimension to 'aberration'. It is the woman who is deeply conscious of all the inequality and injustice in the society and who has been its victim yet she has no complaint against it, not because she has a moral core to give her strength but because she has learnt to manipulate this social system to her advantage. She has instinctively known that it is a mercantile world where everything is a commodity and if you know the tricks of the trade you can obtain success and respectability. We would call it 'Moll Flanders Syndrome after the famous character of Daniel Dofoe[4], the eighteenth century novelist.

Moll Flanders was the daughter of a transported felon. Her mother escaped hanging because she was pregnant. Moll Flanders was brought up in the home for poor girls. Her own life was not virtuous. At one moment she also faced execution for felony and then was transported to Virginia like her mother. But towards the end of her life she returned to England and lived a respectable life with her husband who had also been a transported 'highway man'. Moll herself says :'... We are now grown old; and I am come back to England, being having performed much more than the limited terms of my transportation; and now, notwithstanding all the fatigues and all the miseries we have both gone through, we are both in good heart and health' (*MF* 316).

These words do not show any bitterness because Moll Flanders has learnt the art to manipulate the strings of this mercantile society. This would appear queer in the light of the important incidents of her life which the title sums up :

> The Fortunes and Misfortunes of the famous Moll Flanders, who was born in Newgate, and during a life of continued variety, for three score years, besides her childhood, was twelve years a whose five times a wife (where of once to her own brother) twelve years a thief, eight years a transported felon in Virginia at last grew rich, lived honest ... (*MF* 23).

In spite of all these things Moll was able to obtain respectablity because she had found out how the system operates. For, to manipulate any system the first thing that is required is a knowledge of how it works. Moll had learnt that this social system works on a semblance of virtue :

> ... how necessary it is for all women who expect anything in world, to preserve the character of their virtue, even when perhaps they may have sacrificed the thing itself. (*MF* 137)

This was what she had learnt about 'virtue'. She also discovered the true place of love especially in relation to matrimony :

> This knowledge I soon learned by experience, viz. that the state of things was altered as to matrimony, that marriages were here the consequence of politic schemes, for forming interests, carrying on business, and that love had no share, or but very little, in the matter (*MF* 74-75).

Marriage is also governed by the law of demand and supply in this mercantile world although the market was unfavourable to women : 'the market ran all on the men's side' (*MF* 75). In business, a businessman has to spot out his prospective customer. Having done this, he has to draw the customer to himself gently and cleverly as a fisherman hooks the fish. It is a sort of battle of wits. If the customer gives the businessman the slip the latter loses. In the event the customer accepts the bargain, he becomes the loser. All these factors operate in the sphere of matrimony also. And Moll can convert all her marriages to her advantage because she has a grasp of these laws:

> I picked out my man without much difficulty by the judgement I made of his way of courting me. I had let him run on with his protestations that he loved me above all the world;...
>
> This was my man ; but I was to try him to the bottom ; and indeed in that consisted my safety, for if he balked, I knew I was undone, as surely as he was undone if he took me (*MF* 84).

For a woman marriage is the game of 'deceiving the deceiver' but many women fail to win only because they have fear :

> I think at this time we suffer most in; it is nothing but lack of courage, ... This, I say, is the woman's snare; but would the ladies once but get above that fear, and manage rightly, they would more certainly avoid it (the state of being an old maid). (*MF* 82)

Even when a woman has been wronged it is not anger but patience --

cool and calculating patience -- that comes to her advantage : '... a woman can never want an opportunity to be revenged of a man that has used her ill, and that there were ways enough to humble such a fellow as that ...' (*MF* 76).

In course of time Moll discovered that the husband whom she had hooked with such skill and with whom she had settled in America was her step-brother. By that time she had a son by him yet she did not feel any sense of guilt at this discovery :

> In the meantime, as I was but too sure of the fact, I lived thereupon in open avowed incest, and whoredom, and all under the appearance of an honest wife, and though I was not much touched with the crime of it, yet the action had something in it shocking to nature, and made my husband even nauseous to me. However, upon the most sedate consideration, I resolved that it was absolutely necessary to conceal it either to mother or husband ; and thus I lived with the greatest pressure imaginable for three years more. (*MF* 94)

Moll had also learnt when to talk and when to keep silent. She met her son, who was now a grown-up lad when she was transported to Virginia. The meting was full of genuine love and affection : "This was the substance of our first day's conversation, the pleasantest day that ever passed over my head in my life, and which gave me the truest satisfaction" (*MF* 312). Yet she concealed that fact from her son that she was a married woman and her husband had come along with her. When her husband (her son's father and her half-brother) died, she lived like a widow and then after some days' absence told her son that she had married again. And, thus, she introudced her husband to her son. But for sometime she let her husband believe that her son was her 'cousin'. It was only after sometime that she told him the truth. She had learnt that even 'truth' has to be revealed in parts even to those who are one's nearest and dearest. This is also a law of a mercantile society.

In everything that Moll did, right since her childhood, her own point of view has been the most important thing for her. Though she truly loves her fifth and the last husband yet she talks about him and his affairs only sparingly because as she says : 'But this is to be my story, not my husband's' (*MF* 314).

It is possible to see Moll either as the 'new woman' or as the modern-woman. Her phrase 'to deceive the deceiver' might attract the advocates of feminism. In a study entitled, *The Divided Mind : Studies in Defoe and Richardson,*[5] Suresh Vaid points out that what Moll Flanders does in the eighteenth century milieu finds vehement support in the statement of the twentieth century feminist, Kate Millet, who says that in a patriarchy, a "female is continually obliged to seek survival or advancement through the approaval of the males as those who hold power. She may do this either through appeasement or through the exchange of her sexuality for support or status" [6] (Millet 54).

But in this study such women characters have been called 'aberrations'. Where characters like Moll Flanders appear in modern Indo-English fiction the present study labels them as 'Moll Flanders Syndrome'. A syndrome indicates a pathology, a sort of morbidity. Oxford English Dictionary defines syndrome as 'The aggregate of signs and symptoms associated with any morbid process'. In the case of Moll Flanders, these are set of response -- patterns which Moll Flanders uses to gain respectability and which have been mentioned earlier. Where a female character uses a set of such techniques to gain respectability in our society which is also a male-dominated society with mercantile morals, and where the woman has no complaint against the society, where she does not want to change or refine the society, it is an indication of some morbidity. That is why this study has used the phrase 'Moll Flanders Syndrome'.

The women characters of Namita Gokhale's second novel, *Gods, Graves and Grandmother* (1994) exemplify this 'Moll Flanders Syndrome'. Ammi was a 'Courtesan', a 'Kothawali,' who was a Muslim by religion. She has been thrown out of her 'Kotha' and she finds herself without any money in a Delhi slum. Yet she manages to obtain not only respectability but a sort of 'sainthood' with a considerable following. She is able to achieve this by cleverly manipulating the social machinery to her own advantage. In some way it resembles the history of Moll Flanders.

Ammi's deftness at the art of 'survival' becomes evident to us the moment we hear of her for the first time in the opening chapter of the novel. Gudiya, her grand-daughter and also the narrator of the story, tells us how her 'resourceful' grandmother steals a marble slab from the building site behind their shanty and places it beneath the 'Peepal tree' along with five 'rounded river stones' and a few marigold flowers to complete the hurriedly improvised shrine. In one go she bids farewell to her past life when as a Kothawali singer, she enjoyed a 'rich' status. Her instinct tells her that in order to manipulate the system she must present a semblance of 'virtue'. In her case 'virtue' means obliterating her past altogether. Here what Ammi does in her new 'role' fully echoes the words of Moll Flanders :

> ... how necessary it is for all women who expect anything in the world to preserve the character of their virtue, even when perhaps they may have sacrificed the thing itself (*MF* 137).

So now as the owner of the newly-created shrine, she becomes an entirely new person. She abandons her 'burqa' and consigns it to her 'trunk along with the sequined ghararas and beaded reticules'. Although never well-versed in the higher tenets of Hinduism, Ammi quickly takes to 'bhajan-singing'. Her 'honeyed-voice' also takes a new texture and she is able to utter "Arre Rama, Rama, Rama", with ease. Very soon her new 'avtaar' starts yeielding results and devotees start thronging the 'shrine' filling her 'thali' with 'coins and notes'.

Ammis's first acid test comes when she is required to 'tackle' Sundar Pahalwan. Sundar Pahalwan is all out to exercise his 'territorial rights over the stretch of pavement' which is being used by Ammi for her 'jhuggi'. In her usual 'honeyed-voice' Ammi tells Sunder Pahalwan, "Seize our money Pahalwanji but spare our self-respect. I am the widow of a Brahmin, my husband was a priest. Guard your tongue or else a virtuous woman's curses may follow you" (*GGG 10*). The Pahalwan is further asked to come the following week and take his 'cash'. But the following Monday Sunder Pahalwan is surprised to find Ammi singing a bhajan in front of 'a statue of Durga astride a tiger' under a 'glittering canopy' with a band of worshippers assembled around the shrine. The result is -- Sunder Pahalwan is completely overpowered and he does not leave the shrine before leaving eleven rupees in the 'Thali'! Similarly, when the man from the Municipal Corporation comes with the demolition order for the 'pucca cement structure' which now houses Ammi and Gudiya he falls at Ammi's feet and begs her forgiveness for the 'blasphemy'.

There also comes a time when, like Moll Flanders, Ammi finds herself on the wrong side of the law. Her fingerprints are found on the 'axe' with which a slum-dweller Saboo has killed another slum-dweller, Shambhu. Amma is led off to the Police Station but the presence of her devotees succeeds in getting her out of the case.

Even Pandit Kailash Shastri, a scholarly person, well-versed in religious rituals, accepts Ammi as his superior in theological and spiritual matters. Ammi achieves this 'miracle' through her resorting to 'silence' and 'vague generalisations'. She meets one of the technical objections of the Pandit in these words : "It is all Lord Krishna's Leela ... Sab Guddi-Gudde Ka Khel Hai ... She has by now perfected the art of presenting confusing abstractions as exalted philosophy, and converted her lack of specific religious knowledge into a gnostic strength" (*GGG* 40-47). And the Pandit is so mesmerized that at one stage he says : "I can sense that she is an extra-ordinary woman with remarkable siddhis ... If even the dust from her mind were to settle on an ordinary mortal like me I would become a better and cleverer person" (*GGG* 53). Thus, Ammi cleverly manipulates Pandit Kailash Shastri into declaring her a 'saintly' person. Of course, it is also in the Pandit's own interest that Ammi should become a 'saint' and draw a large following about her. It is this weakness of Kailash Shastri which Ammi is at once able to perceive through her long experience. Hence, true to the laws of this mercantile society Ammi's 'rise' becomes possible because it serves the mutual interests of both the Pandit and Ammi.

With Phoolwati, Sunder Pahalwan and Pandit Shastri on her side, the temple activity thrives and Ammi is able to achieve her desired end, i.e. turn the temple into a commercially viable venture. Having accomplished her aim, the old lady gradually increases her 'abstraction,' 'detachment' and 'inexplicable remoteness' thereby lending a mystical charm and aura to her personality. Hence, it is not at all surprising that after her death, the Pandit declares that 'she had attained Maha Samadhi by voluntarily relinquishing her consciousness to the large universe'. It is in keeping with such status that she is 'buried in the temple premises in the lotus-position'.

Ammi uses her show of 'virtue' and her 'silence' to successfully manipulate the male-dominated society. She handles Pandit Kailash Shastri by her 'silence' and 'vague generalisations' about theology and Sunder Pahalwan by her show of 'virtue' and piety. Another female character, Phoolwati, the widow of the murdered tea-shop owner Shambhu, uses a different Moll Flanders technique to handle both Sunder Pahalwan and Pandit Kailash Shastri.

With Sunder Pahalwan she uses the art of 'deceiving the deceiver'. After Shambhu's death she realises that to carry on her business she must have a husband. But a widow in a slum running a tea-shop might send out singals that she is a weak creature who can be prevailed upon easily and would make an obedient and disciplined wife. This would be her undoing. So, first as Moll Flanders 'picked out the man' who would be her husband — 'I picked out my man' — Phoolwati also picked out her man, the slum-bully Sunder Pahalwan. But Phoolwati does not let him guess that she is weak but starts bullying the 'bully' at their first encounter :

> Lost your tongue? ... such a Dara Singh hulk of a man, but with the courage of a mouse! Why are you so scared of Phoolwati, man? Will she bite you? Will she eat you up? Arre Bhai, Phoolwati is just a timid woman and you are a hero-wrestler. Just say what you have to say. You want to discuss business with me, don't you? Then say so! Come to my house at seven this evening and we can discuss whatever you want to. (*GGG* 84)

To what extent Phoolwati can dictate her terms becomes further clear when Sunder Pahalwan proposes marriage to her. Like Moll Flanders, Phoolwati too, is aware that in a mercantile society 'marriage-market' is heavily baised in favour of men. Hence, to pre-empt any such move from Sunder Pahalwan's side, Phoolwati gives her consent 'subject to certain conditionalities' :

> These were, firstly, that he would build a pucca house for her, the ownership of which would irrevocably be hers; secondly, that he would allow her to continue running her business as before, and thirdly, that Sundar Pahalwan was to treat me (Gudiya) as their adoptive daughter. (*GGG* 141)

In the milieu of Phoolwati the 'conditionalities', if at all, would come from the male side, but here we find Phoolwati reversing the prevalent norm of the society. She is not an avowed feminist but her practical common sense view of things, coupled with her domineering stature, do bring about this reversal of roles.

Also, she never lets her grip over Sundar Pahalwan slacken. Once when Sundar Pahalwan starts thrashing the driver of the school-bus who has come to pick up Gudiya, Phoolwati lets him go on for some time and then in order to show who is the master begins to scold Sundar for being uncivil to the driver whom she now calls her 'guest' : "You Joker, I called you here at seven, and instead you stroll in any time and beat up my guests. Just who do you think you are, Mr. Wrestler?" (*GGG* 86).

In the case of Pandit Kailash Shastri, Phoolwati, unlike Ammi, does not take the help of 'silence' or 'vague generalisations'. She takes intitative and projects herself to the forefront. After Ammi's death Pandit Kailash Shastri starts delivering 'discourses' on Gita. Phoolwati objects to this : "Forget your philosophy-wilosophy ... only Lata Mangeshkar could replace our Mataji" (*GGG* 94). And then announces that henceforth she would lead the 'bhajans'. Every one dismisses the idea as absurd, for Phoolwati has no musical talents, nor any training in music. Yet she holds her ground and makes her 'debut' :

> From the moment she picked up the mike, she was a star. Her infectious smile, her energy, her optimism, her spontaneity, all communicated themselves to her audience. The off-scale notes did not seem to matter. It was a sort of miracle. (*GGG* 95)

Even the Pandit has to admit that 'the songs went down better than his discourses'.

In one respect Phoolwati even surpasses Moll Flanders. Moll had developed and perfected her technique through her own experience and she used it for her own advantage But Phoolwati succeeds in bringing round another woman, Gudiya, the grand-daughter of Ammi to her point of view about the society and a woman's attitude toward it.

Gudiya develops along the lines in which a good-looking, ambitious and careless slum-girl generally develops. In their dissatisfaction with their surroundings and the ambition to become rich and famous such girls become total wrecks in the end. The reason is they figure themselves as rebels and do not have the patience to study how the social system functions and to learn to manipulate it. In some respects Moll Flanders also thought along these lines when she as a child was being brought up in a charitable institution. She would always say, 'I want to be a gentlewoman.' This is exactly what Gudiya says : "I am going to become a film star and marry the Prime Minister's son... I will be the richest woman in the world..." (*GGG* 99). But whereas Moll Flanders was quick to realise the stupidity of her juvenile ambitions and could grow out of them into a cool and calculating person, Gudiya remains in this world of make-believe as a larva in its cocoon until Phoolwati helps her to come out of this cocoon. In this condition of mind Gudiya fails to grasp the significance of what her grandmother, Ammi had been doing : ... I wanted to be outrageous and wicked -- I wanted above all, to escape from the stifling piety that was enveloping my grandmother' (*GGG* 99).

The route to success through education does not appeal to her. Her admission to Roxanne Lamba's English-medium school does not inculcate any higher ideals in her, nor does she have any desire for 'an impressive career'. She can never associate success with 'studies' -- in fact, she has an abhorrence for all kinds of education. The easiest course for such girls is to use their body to achieve their goal. This is exactly what Gudiya does. During the adolescent stage itself she becomes quite conscious of her beauty and body. She herself tells, "I had developed a figure. My breasts were like torpedoes, and long legs and very small waist. My skin was like my mother's, very fair. I was not, thank goodness, blonde like her, although my hair had a bleached uncared look until Phoolwati took me under her wing" (*GGG* 54).

Such girls do not realise that it is a male-dominated mercantile society and women who seek to trade with this 'commodity' without first mastering the business laws which govern this mercantile society, always find themselves at the brink of precipice which leads them to their ruin. This happens with Gudiya also who sees the prince of her dream in a 'bandwallah', Kalki and is so infatuated with him that she becomes pregnant. She loses all her notions of becoming 'rich' and as the mother of an illegitimate child could have lost her respectability, and since Gudiya happens to be among the inner-circle of those who run the temple, this might have been damaging to these persons — Pandit Kailash Shastri, Phoolwati and Sundar Pahalwan also. It is here that Phoolwati's knowledge of how reputation and moral values operate in this mercantile society comes to Gudiya's aid. It is necessary that the unborn child must have a father so that the child does not have the stigma of illegitimacy. Hence, Phoolwati uses the muscle power of Sundar Pahalwan to force Kalki into marrying Gudiya. She even brings round Pandit Kailash Shastri to this point of view : "And if his (Kalki's) little worm were to crawl into her (Gudiya's) belly, and leave her with a baby in her lap, what will you and I do Panditji?" (*GGG* 125).

Also, Phoolwati advises Gudiya after the marriage that she should consider her husband, Kalki a 'disposable being': "The child will have a legitimate father now. Your Kalki has served his function. You can't waste your time like this, Gudiya, with these bandwallahs." But Gudiya comes to this realisation after some months of an unhappy married life which leaves her a broken woman with all her dreams shattered : "... that this was how my whole life might pass — in indifference, indignities and calculated cruelties" (*GGG* 170). However, the advice of Phoolwati prevails and Kalki is given some money and packed off to

Bombay. It is similar to the case of a man giving his unwanted wife some money and turning her out of his house. It is the same thing with the roles reversed. And in course of time Gudiya all but forgets him, 'I have all but forgotten him.' She starts living in the present : 'It is easy to live in the present'. But she is ready for whatever might come in her way : "... There was nothing about my future I any longer wanted to know. I was ready for whatever came my way ..." (*GGG* 176).

As for her past, she hopes that she will be able to invest it with a 'veil of fabulism and mystery' as her Ammi had successfully done : "When enough time passes, and the dust settles on those troubled memories, perhaps I shall be able to embellish them with a veil of fabulism and mystery. Rendering the past acceptable, if not account-able is a talent I inherited from my Ammi" (*GGG* 181).

Though the novel ends here yet in these words of Gudiya there is a hint of what she might become. Her Ammi had started a new life in the slum. She had been able to give an 'aura' to her past life and died a 'saint' in the eyes of her followers. Gudiya is the grand-daughter of Ammi and might as well repeat the game. For, with the blood of Ammi in her veins and the teaching of Phoolwati to guide her Gudiya — who otherwise would have been shattered by this male-dominated society — might as well be on the road to becoming another Moll Flanders because as she herself says : " The end of the world is nowhere in sight" (*GGG* 181).

NOTES

1. Namita Gokhale, *Paro : Dreams of Passion* (New Delhi : Rupa & Co., 1991). All subsequent references to this edition will be referred to as *Paro*.

2. Ferheiz C. Bharucha, " Namita Gokhale's *Paro : Dreams of Passion*", *Commonwealth Fiction* ed. R. K. Dhawan, 2 Vols. (New Delhi : Classical Publishing House, 1988) 2 : 67.

3. Bharucha 68.

4. Daniel Defoe, *Moll Flanders* (London : Pan Books, 1963). All subsequent references to this edition will be referred to as *MF*.

5. Suresh Vaid, *The Divided Mind : Studies in Defoe and Richardson* (New Delhi : Associated Publishing House, 1979).

6. Kate Millet, *Sexual Politics* (London : Virgo, 1971) 54.

7. Namita Gokhale, *Gods, Graves and Grandmother* (New Delhi : Rupa & Co., 1994). All subsequent references to this edition will be referred to as *GGG*.

CONCLUSION

The four preceding chapters have been detailed considerations of the 'new woman' and its 'aberration' in India fiction in English, through the novels of the authors chosen for the study. The novelists make us feel that it is worth while to try and understand the 'new woman' with the hope that such a scrutiny would at least suggest some of the criteria upon which future studies on woman in contemporary Indian fiction may be made. The aim here has been to objectively present and investigate a woman's consciousness at the moral, emotional and spiritual levels. It also presents the shifts in the general literary sensibility of the period towards the 'new woman'. Thus, it enables us to study the 'new woman' in modern Indian fiction in a critical perspective.

The two novelists, Kamala Markandaya and Anita Desai belong to the same stream. The development of their women characters is along moral and spiritual lines which means commitment to a system of values, the yearning for a life of fulfilment where fulfilment comes when the woman has a value-system and there is also present an environment in which such values can find expression through sharing and participation. It also means an attempt to view the lot of women in the scheme of things with a heart which understands and sympathises and also goes out to everything that is tender, meek and suffering including animals and birds.

In these two novelists, these commitments of the 'new woman' are represented through certain metaphors and images. The questions of economic freedom, social status, security and such things assume a secondary role. As regards the process of development of the ideas of commitment, they first appear in a vague and indistinct form (as in the case of Kamala Markandaya) and later on they become fully established (as in the case of Anita Desai). That is why the women characters of Kamala Markandaya are referred to as 'anticipating the new woman' while those of Anita Desai are called 'new woman proper'.

However, one might expect the female characters of other women novelists who wrote after these to continue this process of development and grapple with more fundamental problems and aspire toward higher ideals of womanhood. But when we come to Shobha De and Namita Gokhale we find that they have deviated from this stream of development and in their novels the women characters, if at all they could be termed 'new women', represent an entirely different value-system. Their concern lies with themselves and they cannot view any thing in the wider perspective. Their endeavours are to set themselves on a position equal to men or even higher. Since most of these women are economically independent and socially emancipated they are tempted to level their scores with men in the present social order. So they even go to the extent of demonstrating that they can not only have their own way in all matters but they can also beat men at their own game of general dominance. For them, men are to be considered a source of enjoyment -- these women characters do not do anything 'new' but merely engage themselves in a metaphorical role-reversal. It is only an attempt on their part to turn the value—system of male-dominated society upside down.

However, in the process of development of art one often comes across such 'sallies' but they are always brief and art returns to the mainstream of spiritual and moral values. So such 'sallies' which might dazzle for a short spell cannot become a different or a parallel stream which branches off from the mainstream and continues its separate course. Hence, the study calls the women characters of Shobha De and Namita Gokhale as 'aberrations'. Here it is worth noting that Shobha De, the first author in this pattern, after her dazzling 'sally' in her earlier four novels, too, acknowledged the need to return to the maintream of writing, evidence of which is to be seen in her *Sultry Days*.

The study of Kamala Markandaya and Anita Desai shows that the 'new woman' is not confined to the self - conscious, emancipated and educated woman. One can come across such a woman in any social environment or in any class of society. Rukmani, despite her poor status and rural background, anticipates the 'new woman' at many levels. Reflecting on the lot of woman, she gives evidence of 'new' thinking on issues such as giving male heir to the family and barrenness. To meet these situations she also evolves her own set of responses or defense-mechanism. A similar approach is adopted by the vegetable-seller. She, too, resorts to defense-mechanism to put up with her single status. Thus, both Rukmani and the vegetable-seller are able to reflect on and identify with the lot of woman in general. The woman in Rukmani is also able to perceive that a woman wants something more than material comforts. She understands what Muslim women miss moving 'vieled in bourkas'. To her, this amounts to denying an individual the freshness of life — it is a great impediment in the realisation of an individual's spiritual needs.

But when we turn to Shobha De and Namita Gokhale, the women characters seldom give evidence of such thinking. Karuna abhors the society of women of middle and lower class -- she has contempt for their small 'concerns'. Priya also feels uncomfortable with her middle-class suburban existence. Both Paro and Priya make an attempt to shake off the shackles of social conventions and try to liberate themselves from their middle class pseudo-morality in order to break themselves free from male-dominance. In the process Paro alone is able loosen herself completely from the shackles of social conventions. Priya does not reach the same level of 'emancipation' as Paro does. Thus, the concerns of Karuna, Paro and Priya do not extend beyond 'I am the good thing'. It is only when Nisha has some inkling of her 'commitments' that she is able to identify herself with the women of middle-class and their problems. Unlike Karuna her attitude is not one of hatred but of fellow-feeling.

The 'new woman' not only reflects on the lot of woman but also understands and sympathises with everything that is tender, meek and suffering including the animals and birds. The sight of injured baby-monkey hurts the sensibility of young Saroja. Through it, she sympathises with the weak and the suffering. The death of Maya's pet Toto triggers off a set of responses. Her attitude to the death of the pup is the metaphor of tenderness, innocence and its death, therefore, touches the basic sympathies which lie at the core of her heart. Sita's desperate attempt to frighten away the crows who are bent upon killing a fallen eagle touchingly exemplifies her sensitive and tender response to anything that is harsh and brutal. But no such feeling is to be seen in Karuna and Anjali when the two talk about the death of two pigeons left under the latter's charge by 'Babaji'. Their gesture is one of casualness and indifference.

The 'new woman' also shows similar feelings for the unborn child. In Saroja's case the feelings of compassion for fellow-sufferers get transferred from the beasts to the unborn child. Saroja finds the idea of abortion abhorring. Over the issue of abortion the sensibilties of the two sisters, Saroja and Lalitha are hurt. They fumble for some kind of solution but there is no remorse for the act. The crux of the discussion revolves round the human aspect, i.e. a life being snuffed out and the entire experience of abortion. Sita wants the miracle of not giving birth — she even questions whether child-birth is an act of creation or a violent pain-stricken act that destroys everything what is safely contained in the womb by releasing it into a murderous world. As opposed to the views of Saroja and Lalitha on the issue of abortion, Karuna's attitude is directed towards herself. It never allows her to think of the unborn child.

The 'new women' have deep commitments to spiritual concerns, sharing and companionship based on understanding and sympathy, need for a sensitive approach in others towards themselves to understand their emotional and spiritual needs, attempt to understand others' point of view and the like. For Maya, meaning and fulfilment in life come through tenderness, mutual sharing and commitment to deeper things. To Sita fulfilment implies appreciation of her tender, delicate feelings and emotions and a throbbing life of consciousness, she demands a sensitive approach in others towards herself. Nanda Kaul realises that her relations cannot offer either emotional or spiritual sustenance. Hence, she shuts herself from all relations and withdraws into her own shell. Her commitment is to her withdrawal. She seeks fulfilment in this sense. For Bim the house with all its associations becomes an essential and inalienable part of her personality. She begins to consider the circumscribing nature of the house as something ideal.

Under the category 'aberration' also the women occasionally talk of the necessity of commitment in life but since they are not committed to any ideal their commitments appear to be pseudo-commitments. Karuna talks of 'commitment' and being in the 'mainstream' but this 'commitment', too, is some kind of an 'aberration'. Even her intellectual pursuits suggest that she is incapable of involving herself in something serious. To find meaning in life and to 'know' herself Paro takes to play— acting but her flirtation with the art form (play-acting) is as momentary as her 'one-night stands.' Like Paro, Priya also feels the urge to look for something deeper — she takes to 'reading' for sometime but since it is not linked to the core of her personality, it remains only a time-killing hobby.

Out of all the women characters of Shobha De and Namita Gokhale, there are only two women, Nisha and Pramila who are able to discover some 'commitment' in their life and give it a meaning. Nisha begins to discover her commitments by simply not becoming a part of God's pseudo--commitments. Her 'commitment' towards the end of the novel emerges as a commitment to a cause — she exposes Yashwantbhai through her write-ups and remains undeterred despite Deb's warning to keep off. In the end Pramila also finds a 'cause'. She joins the movement which seeks to expose persons like Yashwantbhai. This changes her life and she returns to her 'roots'. Pramila's experience sums up in a nutshell the course charted by women characters whom we have called 'aberrations'. It shows that the only ray of hope for such women is to return to their roots and join the mainstream.

The consciousness of their commitment enables the 'new women' to perceive the moral shallowness of the people around them. Maya realises quite early that her husband is pragmatic, intelligent, patronising but devoid of any commitment. Sita associates dull safe routine with Raman and finds that he can neither travel with her mentally nor emotionally. To Nanda Kaul, the pragmatism of her husband never touches the core of her personality.

The study also points out paradigms of modern women but they remain at the periphery of a 'new woman's personality ; none of them reaches the core of her personality. Nearly all of them are socially emancipated and have modern outlooks. Maya's mother-in-law and Pratimaben are examples of women who are dedicated to the social cause. Nila's case is that of a woman who is fighting her divorce case in a court of law and trying to be independent. Also, we have Leila, the Persian lecturer, who has married a tubercular patient purely for love and finally there is Pom, modern yet traditional woman who surrenders before her mother-in-law when the question of the birth of a son comes up and starts going to the temple to achieve this end. All these paradigms are there but none of these women can understand the deeper emotional and spiritual needs of the 'new woman' Similarly, the desciption of women in the 'New Women' category with MBA degrees, wearing business suits and insisting on being addressed as Ms and with whom workaholism has become a fashionable word does not get the approval of Nisha in *Sultry Days*. To her, the lives of such women lack depth and a sense of purpose and hence are not worth emulating. But there is another category, that of single women whose description by Nisha is of considerable significance. Such women complain of a 'void' in their lives. It is an emotional and spiritual 'void' they talk about. Unlike Karuna, these women at least give evidence of the consciousness of such a 'void' in their lives.

When the 'new woman' describes her commitments or views her position in the scheme of things, she uses certain metaphors and images. They also serve as a projection of her sensibility and values. Saroja is able to understand the scheme of relationships as they exist in this male-dominated society through the metaphor of dominance. The example of the 'beasts of burden', for whom she is filled with sympathy, is used for this purpose. It is basically the woman inside her considering the predicament as the lot of woman where man is the dispensr. The idea of dominance leads to feelings of compassion for fellow—sufferers — first it is the beasts and later on it gets transferred to the unborn child. Maya looks for a life of total fulfilment in the image of the moon. It is the dominant metaphor in the novel. It represents the life of fulfilment at all levels of her psyche. Maya's awareness of her spiritual needs is reflected in her attitude to the cabaret dancing-girls. It gets connected to the dancing bears in her dream. They represent tenderness, innocence and persecution. Thus, Maya, with her sensibility, identifies her suffering through the metaphor of persecution. Also, in Maya's case the 'cry' of the peacock is a metaphor which stands for ecstasy, sharing, companionship which alone mean fulfilment and it is for this that she yearns. Sita, who finds the world around her exulting in destruction, views her position through the metaphor of violence. She resorts to 'escape' and in her case the 'island' becomes the metaphor of escape. In Nanda Kaul's case the dominant metaphor is barrenness. The attempt to escape barrenness brings destruction. For Bim, the house is a metaphor. It is some kind of a shell out of which she refuses to 'come out'. Leaving it would mean splitting her personality. So it becomes the symbol of her circumscribing mentality.

The realisation of fulfilment becomes an important aspect of a 'new woman's personality. Rukmani achieves some kind of fulfilment in her relationship with Kenny. It is a part of desire in every individual to call something one's own. She neither considers the relationship immoral nor does she suffer from any inner conflict. It is a relationship based on human bonds with companionship and sharing as its chief elements and hence cause no embarrassment to her. Also, it is a relationship beyond the moral and social code of the traditional woman. Not sharing it with anyone is only an urge to assert her individuality as a person and as a woman.

For a 'new woman' deeper meaning in life is realised when her emotional and spiritual needs get recognition instead of the socially accepted ones of security, comfort and respectability. But more often than not the pragmatic approach of the persons around her fails to fathom the depth of a 'new woman's' psyche, for this approach measures everything in terms of material or worldly success. This happens in the case of Maya and Sita also. But since the commitment of these women to a full and meaningful life is both deep and conscious, they can recognize the true ring of such a life even if they might have a fleeting glimpse of it. Maya can see it in the scene of the husband, wife and the dog and is quick to perceive how all the three share this bond. The moment embodies the elements which Maya seeks in love and in marriage — a feeling of tenderness, understanding, sharing and companionship. Sita sees it in the image of the old man devotedly attending on his dying tubercular wife in a park. It is her own vision of perfect harmony between a man and a woman, an example of mutually shared love and understanding. It is the perception of this feeling at the core which makes the incident so significant in Sita's consciousness.

Bim realises that the true meaning of being can be achieved through 'love' and not 'rejection'. She breaks the barriers of her circumscribing mentality and 'comes out' of the 'cocoon-house'. In this new insight she feels liberated from her narrow mentality and accepts those who had moved 'out'. She realises that together they form a perfect whole. The widening of the mental horizon results in doing away with the bitterness. Thus, Bim achieves spiritual wholeness by consciously choosing to bridge the rift with others which also enables her to find her own life's relevance. It is this inclusive vision of the self's affiliation with the family and society that enriches the experience, hamonises the self's connections with the family and society and makes the self bathe in "clear light of day".

Physical relationship to, a 'new woman' is a means to higher fulfilment. For Rukmani, physical relationship with her husband is a sort of fulfilment both at the emotional and spiritual levels. It is a part of the core element of every woman's personality, traditional or modern. Maya emphasizes the importance of closeness and bodily contact with her husband, for 'contact' leads to 'communion'. Even in sexual matters outside the marital context the 'new woman' shows her emotional equipoise and moral balance. The aftermath of the near-incestuous encounter between Jayamma and Ravi is important because it gives insight into the moral aspect of the incident. Jayamma does not consider the 'act' immoral. Also, it is not something to be gloated over merely because it is illicit, nor does it become the starting point of an illicit relationship. It does not leave an iota of mark on her phyche. Her response is ethically neutral. Through this incident Jayamma merely acknowledges the fact that there are moments like this in a woman's life and such moments should not disturb the emotional equipoise and moral balance of the woman. The 'new woman' is able to reconcile such conflicting issues as illegitimacy, aborting an illegitimate child, moments of near-incest and the like. Her approach towards these situations is that she does not need to be a rebel, nor does she require a cushion to absorb the shock. At the core she has that moral strength which expresses itself at the surface as her equipoise. Ira, Lalitha possess this equipoise in ample measure.

Unlike Rukmani and Maya, Karuna experiences no such fulfilment in her relationship with her husband. Their love making too, is a listless and a mechanical affair. This is in sharp contrast to what Shobha De herself says in her book *Uncertain Liaisons:* — "With ignorance levels rapidly dropping, chances are we will walk into a new era of enlightened, evolved sexual relations. The 'act' in future may well be viewed as something more meaningful than mere mating or animal copulation" (De 208). But the experience of her women characters suggests just the opposite - the 'act' is not at all 'meaningful', it is mere 'mating' or 'animal copulation'. Although Paro's sexual adventures liberate her from marriage and convention — the liberation remains only at the periphery. This has led Bachi J. Karkaria to conclude that "if liberation is going to be just one-up womanship, and titillation the only end of a finally outed sexuality, I'd rather stay buckled to the chastity belt"[2] (Karkaria 2).

Marriage as such is not an issue with the 'new woman'. The 'new woman' neither seeks fulfilment in marriage nor through marriage. The 'new women' have deep commitments to certain ideals and since their male-cunterparts lack in commitments to such ideals, it becomes a cause of tension. But the cause of tension is not marriage or the institution of marriage as such. Husband, though the most important part of any marital relationship, just becomes a part of the people around them; he ceases to be a distinct entity. He is just an element in the larger set of people around them. Maya is not unhappy with her marriage as such. For Nanda Kaul all relationships of her marital state remain at the periphery and because of her deep commitment she needs no outside help. Sita finds meaninglessness in marriage right from the beginning. Even after the 'escape' she realises that she will have to put up with meaningless relationships of marital life and continue life along with it. But she does not give up her basic commitment. Towards the end of the novel Bim comes to realise that the true meaning of being can be realised not only through putting up with others, it lies in the acceptance and appreciation of others' point of view. Hence, the experiences of Maya, Sita, Nanda Kaul and Bim suggest that there is no relevance of a 'new woman's attitude to marriage. In her case marriage only becomes the occasion to reveal the deeper difference of approach towards the more fundamental and spiritual issues.

As opposed to this, marriage is a kind of obsession with women like Karuna and others included in the category "aberrations". They hate having a husband, yet they must have one. They want one under the roof, may be as a stranger with whom they can spring up occasional confrontation. Both Karuna and Priya remain stuck up in a 'meaningless marriage'. The women of this type put up with a stranger-husband, not out of choice or conviction, they need one to afford the luxuries of life. In their second marriages both Anjali and Paro put up with their homosexual husbands for the same reason. A husband is also needed to be shown to every one as one who has been 'conquered'. Ritu and Priya demonstrate this in their married life. Examples of women like Ritu are not common and often the wife has to demean herself as a woman, as a person and also as a human-being. Anjali puts up with Abe's 'seductions'. She even turns a blind eye to her second husband, Kumar's 'affair' with his homosexual partner, Murty. Such women also put up with male-violence. Gul's manhandling of Ritu is an example of this.

For these women, marriage also enables them to indulge in adultery. Since 'one-man-for-one-woman' norm does not seem to exist in their society, extra-marital affairs and 'casual-flings' are not considered extra ordinary things. For Paro, marriage is something which cannot be treated as permanent. Hence, after her first marriage, she lives in open adultery. Both Karuna and Priya involve themselves in extra-marital relationships with no feelings of guilt attached. How a marriage counsellor looks at this problem is stated by Shobha De in her book *Uncertain Liaisons:* "My Clients are more liberal. Adultery is still a big issue, of course. But it does n't destroy marriage as it once used to" [3] (De 14). In the same essay an attractive socialite echoes the marriage counsellor's words : "My friends and I love our husbands. Our affairs have nothing to do with marriage. We believe our relationships are strong enough. In any case — if he can stray, so can we. That much is clearly understood. There are more important aspects to marriage. Children, financial security ... it's unrealistic to expect two people to remain faithful in today's context. It's almost absured" [4] (De 14). Thus, it becomes clear that for the majority of women covered under "aberrations" the value of family and marriage is undermined and the traditional concept of marriage with fidelity as its cardinal principle stands discarded. "The new definition of the marriage postulates complete sexual freedom, with no notion of marital fidelity. Economic security for wife seems to be the cornerstone of this marriage arrangement which appears more like a contract than a vibrant, living, emotional relatonship"[5] (Chandra 244). Devoid of emotional warmth and entered into for expediency, such marriages often break down, leading to divorce and sundering of family ties.

The idea of dominance also occupies an important place in the lives of women of all types. It connotes a different set of meanings to different types of women. The 'new woman' in Saroja views the position of woman in a male-dominated society through the metaphor of dominance. Thus, dominance is seen as part of the scheme of relationships as they exist in a male-made social order where man is the dispenser. Jayamma uses her dominance to run the household — it is not to vindicate herself on the male sex. Had it been so, she would not have nursed her dying husband for whom she had no love. Even in these moments her womanliness does not leave her.

But in the case of "aberrations" the idea of dominance assumes a different meaning. The women in this group think that they can not only have their way in all matters but they can also beat men in the game of gender dominance. Ritu, Asha Rani, Paro and Priya play this 'game'. These women remain obsessed with men. They know to what extent men are to be cultivated and when it is the right moment to drop them. 'Beating men at their own game' is the strategy adopted by Asha Rani to 'use' persons like Amirchand, Suhas and Kishenbhai. Ritu is well-known for her power over men. Paro's sex-adventure spree is also an example of paying back man in his own coin. Priya loses her virginity before marriage but it does not give rise to any apprehension on her part that her husband might find it out. It is her way of turning the value-system of male-dominated society upside down.

Majority of the women characters covered under "aberrations" experience a sense of revolt, they are rebeles who either rebel against the shackles of male-dominated social order or are at least aware of it. Karuna, Anjali, Ritu, Asha Rani, Paro and Priya, despite their commitment to themselves, have some sort of dissatisfaction with the society and its man-made laws. But there is another dimension to 'aberration'. It is the woman who is deeply conscious of all the inequality and injustice in the society and who has been its victim yet she has no complaint against it, not because she has a moral core to give her strength but because she has learnt to manipulate the social system to her advantage. She has instinctively known that it is a mercantile world and if you know the tricks of the trade you can obtain success and respectability. The study calls it 'Moll Flanders Syndrome'.

Where a female character uses a set of response patterns as used by Moll Flanders to gain respectability in our society which is also a male-dominated society with mercantile morals, and where the woman has no complaint against the society, where she does not want to change or refine the society, it is an indication of some morbidity. So the study uses the phrase 'Moll Flanders Syndrome'. Ammi, in some way resembles the history of Moll Flanders. She uses her show of 'virtue' and 'silence' to manipulate the male-dominated society. Phoolwati uses a different Moll Flanders technique. With Sunder Pahalwan she uses the art of 'deceiving the deceiver' and tackles Pandit Kailash Shastri by taking initiative and projecting herself to the forefront. In one respect she even surpasses Moll Flanders. Moll had developed and perfected her technique through her own experience and she used it to her own advantage. But Phoolwati succeeds in bringing round Gudiya to her point of view and a woman's attitude toward it. Phoolwati's knowledge of how reputation and moral values operate in this mercantile society come to Guidya's aid. By the end of the novel we find that with the blood of Ammi and the guidance of Phoolwati on her side, Gudiya is another Moll Flanders in the making.

A fact which deserves special mention with regard to the 'new women proper' of Anita Desai is that theirs is not always a success story similar to that of Karuna. But they do reveal some kind of progression in terms of meaning and fulfilment. Maya may not have achieved success in this sense but her failure does not in any way invalidate her urge for emotional and spiritual needs. After the 'escape' Sita returns with a new insight, a new awareness. She returns because she thinks that inspite of the attitude of the society, the 'new woman' must not escape from it. But in the case of Nanda Kaul no such change takes place - she remains committed to her withdrawal till the end. Bim becomes the 'new woman' when she breaks the barriers of her circumscribing mentality and 'comes out'. Thus, both Sita and Bim realise that neither 'escape' nor 'withdrawing into one's shell' is the answer to a meaningful existence. Withdrawal would mean a negation of this as it happens in the case of Nanda Kaul. The inner-self must not be something that is circumscribing otherwise it will be a 'cocoon' which the 'island' and the 'house' temporarily become for Sita and Bim. The real fulfilment comes when the 'cocoons' of the 'island' and the 'house' are broken. Here it needs to be emphasized that in this journey of fulfilment what Sita achieves is only partial success. She returns and makes a compromise with her situation, though, of course, with a new perception. But Bim goes a step further. She not only comes out of her shell but also realises that the true meaning of life lies in accepting and appreciating others' point of view. So out of all the heroines of Anita Desai it is only Bim who "has created a space which she wishes to occupy, and when she is sure of it she does n't mind visitors or intruders"[6] (Jain 35).

In what direction will such a study lead? The study points out that creative literature should proceed in a direction where there is an opportunity for a woman to realise herself fully — where there is total recognition of her emotional and spiritual needs. This would demand a re-ordering of all social relationships, especially that of husband and wife. It has been seen that nearly all the woman protagonists of Anita Desai's fiction, whom the study calls the 'new women proper', enjoy security, respectability and economic independence but there is a near-total absence of recognition of their deeper and hence more basic needs in their male counterparts. This would not be achieved by bringing about equality of the sexes, or by according women with more power or even by reversing the power structure as it exists in the male-dominated society, hints of which are thrown in the fiction of Shobha De and Namita Gokhale. This would require a total re-ordering of all kinds of realtionships. In such a scheme of things, things like promiscuity and permisiveness would have no place and economic independence or independence of females in all respects would be a natural by-product. But all creative literature should move along these lines as its philosophic base.

Since the study seeks to emphasize the female experience, it may turn out to be a feminist critique with the final aim being to set right the lopsided value-system of culture which serves male--interests. It follows that future literature on women must augment consciousness-raising by providing "realistic insights into female personality development, self perception, interpersonal relationships and other 'private' or 'internal' forms of sexism"[7] (Gorrez 98). The true magnitude of the studies on the woman would be measured in the years to come by the realisation they give to women—that they need not compete with anyone, that all they have to do is to march hand in hand with man and go forward as equal partners, reaching out for an equitable share of man's worldly and spiritual goods, sharing experiences and aspirations.

NOTES

1. Shobha De, "Everybody Needs Sex", *Uncertain Liaisons* ed. Kushwant Singh and Shobha De (New Delhi : Viking Penguin India, 1993) 208.

2. Bachi J. Karkaria, "The Importance of Being Nikki Bedi," *Times of India* 16 Apr. 1995 : 8.

3. Shobha De, "Sex in the Time of Stress", *Uncertain Liaisons* ed. Kushwant Singh and Shobha de (New Delhi : Viking Penguin India, 1993) 14.

4. De 14.

5. Subhash Chandra, "Family and Marriage in Shobha De's *Socialite Evenings*" *Indian Women Novelists* ed. R. K. Dhawan (New Delhi: Sterling Publishers, 1990) 244.

6. Jasbir Jain, "Gender and Narrative Strategy", *Between Spaces of Silence* ed. Kamini Dinesh (New Delhi : Sterling Publishers, 1994) 35.

7. Christine Gorrez, "Exploring the Possibilites of Feminist Literary Criticism on Indian Writing in English", *Indian Women Novelists* ed. R. K. Dhawan (New Delhi : Sterling Publishers, 1990) 98.

BIBLIOGRAPHY

PRIMARY SOURCES

De, Shobha. *Socialite Evenings*. New Delhi : Penguin Books, 1989.

———. *Starry Nights*. New Delhi : Penguin Books, 1991.

———. *Sultry Days*. New Delhi : Penguin Books, 1994.

Desai, Anita. *Cry, The Peacock*. New Delhi : Orient Paperbacks, 1990.

———. *Where Shall We Go This Summer?* New Delhi : Orient paperbacks, 1991.

———. *Fire on the Mountain*. New York : Penguin Books, 1981.

———. *Clear Light of Day*. London : Penguin Books, 1980.

Gokhale, Namita. *Paro : Dreams of Passion*. New Delhi : Rupa & Co., 1991.

———. *Gods. Graves and Grandmother*. New Delhi :Rupa & Co., 1994.

Markandaya, Kamala. *Nectar in a Sieve*. New Delhi : Jaico Publishing House, 1992.

———. *Two Virgins*. New Delhi : Vikas Publishing House, 1977.

———. *A Handful of Rice*. New Delhi : Orient Paperbacks, 1985.

SECONDARY SOURCES

A. BOOKS

Das, Kamla. *My Story*. New Delhi : Sterling Publishers, 1977.

De, Shobha. *Shooting From the Hip*. New Delhi : U.B.S. Publishers, 1994.

Defoe, Daniel. *Moll Flanders*. London : Pan Books, 1963.

Firestone, Shulamith. *The Dialectic of Sex*. New York : Bantam, 1970.

Freidan, Betty. *The Second Stage.* New York : Summit Books, 1981.

Goyal, Bhagwat S. *Culture and Commitment : Aspects of Indian Literature in English.* Meerut : Shalabh Book House, 1984.

Homer. *The Iliad of Homer* Trans. Samuel Butler. Ed. Louise Ropes Loomis. New York : Classic Club, 1942.

Ibsen, Henrick. *A Doll's House.* Trans. Archer et al. Ed. Francis Bull. London : Centenary, 1963.

Iyengar, K. S. Sriniwas. *Indian Writing in English.* Bombay : Asia Publishers, 1987.

Jain, Jasbir. *Stairs to the Attic.* Jaipur : Printwell Publishers, 1987.

Joseph, Margaret P. *Kamala Markandaya.* New Delhi : Arnold Heinemann, 1980.

Krishnaswamy, Shantha. *The Woman in Indian Fiction in English.* New Delhi : Ashish Publishing House, 1984.

Larson, Charles. R. *Fiction in Third World.* Washington, D. C. : Inscape Publishers, 1976.

Mahle, H. S. *Indo-Anglian Fiction : Some Perspectives.* New Delhi : Jainsons Publications, 1976.

Marlow, Christopher. *Doctor Faustus.* Ed. Kitty Datta, Delhi O.U.P., 1980.

Millet, Kate. *Sexual Politics.* London : Virgo, 1972.

Mukherjee, Meenakshi. *The Twice Born Fiction : Themes and Techniques of the Indian Novel in English.* New Delhi : Arnold-Heinemann, 1971.

Parikh, Indira and Pulin K. Garg. *Indian Women : An Inner Dialogue.* New Delhi : Sage Publications, 1989.

Pritam, Amrita. *Raseedi Ticket.* New Delhi : Kitabghar, 1993.

Shirwadkar, Meena. *Image of Woman in the Indo-Anglian Novel.* New Delhi : Sterling Publishers, 1979.

Showalter, Elaine. *A Literatue of Their Own : British Women Novelists from Bronte to Lessing.* Princeton, N. J. : Princeton University Press, 1977.

Singh, Kushwant, and Shobha De, eds. *Uncertain Liaisons.* New Delhi : Viking India Press, 1993.

Vaid, Suresh. *The Divided Mind : Studies in Defoe and Richardson.* New Delhi : Associated Publishing House, 1979.

Wadkar, Hansa. *Sangtye Aika.* Pune : Rajhans Prakashak, 1993.

B. ARTICLES

Acharya, Shanta. "Problems of the Self in the Novels of Anita Desai". *Indian*

Women Noveelists. Ed. R. K. Dhawan. New Delhi : Prestige Books, 1990. 50-67.

Asnani, Shyam. " New Morality in the Modern Indo-English Novel". *Indian Women Novelists.* Ed. R. K. Dhawan. New Delhi : Prestige Books, 1990, 66-69.

Belliappa, Meena "East-West Encounter : Indian Women Writers of Fiction in English". *Fiction and the Reading Public in India.* Ed. C. D. Narasimaiah. Mysore : University Press of Mysore, 1967. 18-27.

Betty and Theodore Roszak. " 'Red Stockings' Manifesto" *Masculine/Feminine.* New York : Harper and Row, 1969 273-276.

Bhargav, Simran and Madhu Jain. "Married Women : Changing Sexuality". *India Today* 15 October 1989 : 154-62.

Bharucha, Ferheiz C. "Namita Gokhale's *Paro : Dreams of Passion* : Meaning through Mediocrity" . *Commonwealth Fiction.* Ed. R. K. Dhawan 2 Vols. New Delhi : Classical Publishing Company, 1988. 2 : 67-72.

Bhaskar, C. I. "Jet-Set Indian Style". Rev. of *Paro : Dreams of Passion,* by Namita Gokhale. *Financial Express* 6 May 1984 : 5.

Bobb, Dilip. "Erogenous Zones". Rev. of *Paro : Dreams of Passion,* by Namita Gokhale. *India Today* 15 Feb. 1984 : 147.

Chandra, Subhash. "Family and Marriage in Shobha De's *Socialite Evenings".* *Indian Women Novelists.* Ed. R. K. Dhawan. New Delhi : Prestige Books, 1990. 244-48.

Couto, Maria. "Multicultural Voices". Rev. of *Paro : Dreams of Passion,* by Namita Gokhale. *Express Magazine* 25 Mar. 1984 : 5.

Cunningham, Gail. Introduction. *The New Woman and the Victorian Novel.* By Cunningham. London : Macmillan Press, 1978. 1-19.

De, Shobha. "Everybody Needs Sex". *Uncertain Liasions.* Ed. Kushwant Singh and Shobha De. New Delhi : Viking Penguin India, 1993. 208-10.

——. "Sex in the Time of Stress". *Uncertain Liasions.* Ed. Kushwant Singh and Shobha De. New Delhi : Viking Penguin India, 1993. 14-17.

Desai, Anita. "Replies to a Questionnaire". *Kakatya Journal of English Studies,* 2nd ser. 4 (Aug. 1981) : 1-4.

——. "Women Writers". *Quest* 65 (April/June 1970) : 40-43. Dwyer, Rachel. "A de in the life of Popular Culture". *Indian Express* 5 Aug. 1995 : 2.

Even, Sarah Jane, Rev. of *Paro : Dreams of Passion,* by Namita Gokhale. *Publishing News* 18 February 1984 : Cols. 2-3.

Freidian, Betty. "Our Revolution is Unique". *Voices of the New Feminism.* Ed. Marry Lou Thompson. Boston : Beacon, 1970. 36-46.

Garg, Ajita. "Women Doubly Ensalved". *Social Welfare (M)* 35.5 (Aug. 1988) : 24-27.

Geetha, P. "The Novels of Kamala Markandaya : Reassessing Feminine Indentity" *Between Spaces of Silence.* Ed. Kamini Dinesh. New Delhi : Prestige Books, 1994. 126-29.

———. "Images and Archetypes in Kamala Markandaya's Novels : A Study in Cultural Ambivalence". *Journal of Commonwealtth Literature* 14.2 (1991) : 169-78.

Ghosh, Biswadeep. "Learning Shobha De in Bombay". *Indian Express* 5 Aug. 1994 : 8.

Gorrez, Christine. "Exploring the Possibilities of Feminist Literary Criticism on Indian Writing in English".*Indian Women Novelists.* Ed. R. K. Dhawan. New Delhi : Prestige Books, 1990 : 98-100.

Heiburn, Carolyn G. "Marriage and Contemporary Fiction" *Critical Quarterly* 5th Ser. 2 (Winter 1978) : 309.

Hoskote, Ranjit. "The Dawning of the New De". *Times of India* 2 Feb. 1995 : 8.

Jain, Jasbir. "In Pursuit of Wholeness : Transcendence of the self in the Novels of Anita Desai" . *Studies in Contemprorary Indian Fiction in English.* Ed. A. N. Dwvedi. Allahabad : Kitab Mahal, 1987. 298-308.

———. "Gender and Narrative Strategy". *Between Spaces of Silence.* Ed. Kamini Dinesh. New Delhi : Prestige Books, 1994, 29-36.

Jain, Madhu. "Psst ....! Corny, Porny, Horny". Rev. of *Starry Nights,* by Shobha De. *India Today* 15 July, 1991 : 140.

Juneja, Renu. "Identity and Femininity in Anita Desai's Fiction". *Journal of South Asian Literature* 22.1 (Summer/Fall 1987) : 72-79.

Karkaria, Bachi J. "The Importance of being Nikki Bedi". *Times of India* 16 Apr. 1995 :8.

Khanna, S.M. "Existentialist Overtones in Anita Desai's *Fire On The Mountain". Indian fiction in English : Problems and Promises.* Ed. R. S. Singh, New Delhi : Barhi Publishers, 1983. 130-137.

Marx and Engels. "The Origin of Family, Private Property and State". *Selected Works.* Moscow : Progress Publishers, 1982. 480-499.

May, Keith M. "New Women". *Characters of Women in Narrative Literature.* London : Macmillan, 181. 105-127.

Mazumdar, S. "Porno, not Creativity". Rev. of *Paro : Dreams of Passion,* by Namita Gokhale. *London Magazine* 9 Feb. 1984 : 99-101.

Mitchell, Juliet. "Women - The Longest Revolution". From Feminism to

Liberation. Cambridge Mass : Schekman, 1971. 120-127.

Nandakumar, Prema. "Sombre the Shadows and Sudden the Lights : A study of Anita Desai's Novels". *Perspectives of Indian Fiction in English.* Ed. M. K. naik. New Delhi : Abhinav Publications, 1985. 174-199.

Nanporia, N. J. "Synthetic Agonies". Rev. of *Paro : Dreams of Passion* by Namita Gokhale. *Times of India* 23 Apr. 1984 : 8.

Narasimhaiah, C. D. "Women in Fiction and Fiction by Women — An Introductory Talk". *The Literary Criterion* 20.4 (1985) : 1-19.

Panigrahi, Bipin B. "Self Apprehension and Self-Identity in *Clear Light of Day" The New Indian Novel in English : A Study of the 1980s.* Ed. Viney Kirpal. New Delhi : Allied Publishers, 1990. 73-81.

Parasuram, Laxmi. " *Fire on the Mountain* : A New Dimension of Feminine Self Perception". *The Literary Criterion* 16.3 (1981) : 58-74.

Patil, P.F. "The Theme of Marital Disharmony in the Novels of Anita Desai". *Indian Women Novelists.* Ed. R. K. Dhawan. New Delhi : Prestige Books, 1990 : 126-142.

Poovaya, Nimmie. "The Emergence of the Feminist Consciousness in Margaret Atwood's *Surfacing* and Anita Desai's *Where Shall We Go This Summer?".* Ccmmonwealth Literature : Problems of Response. Ed. C. D. Narasimhaiah. Bombay : Macmillan India Limited, 1981. 210-217.

Prasad, V.V.N. Rajendra. "Anita Desai and the Wounded Self". *Indian Women Novelists.* Ed. R. K. Dhawan. New Delhi : Prestige Books , 1990. 80-100.

Radhakrishhanan, N. "Alienation and Crisis of Identity". *Indo-Anglian Fiction : Major Treends and Themes.* Madras : Emerald Publishers, 1984. 132-154.

Ram, Atma. "An Interview with Anita Desai". *Interviews with Indian English Writers.* Calcutta : Writers Workshop, 1983. 26-34.

Ramamurthi, K. S. " Kamala Markandaya's *Two Virgins* — A Problem Novel". *Literary Critic* 13.7 (Dec 1981) : 38-45

Rao, C. Vimla. "The Achievement of the Indian Women Novelists". *Indian Literature of the Past Fifty Years (1917 1967).* Ed. C. D. Narasimhaiah. Mysore : University of Mysore, 1970. 213-224.

Roa, K.S. N. "Love, Sex, Marriage and Morality in Kamala Markandaya's Novels". *The Osmania Journal of English Studies* 10 (1973) : 69-77.

Rossenwasser, Ruth K. "Voices of Dissent : Heroines in the Novel of Anita Desai". *Journal of South Asian Literature* 24.2 (Summer/Fall 1984) 101-107.

Sen, Nabaneeta Dev. "Man, Woman and Fiction". *The Literary Criterion* 20.4 (1985) : 91—101.

Sengupta, Ranjana. "Siblings Ribaldry". Rev. of *Sisters*, by Shobha De. *The Times of India* 26 Apr. 1992 : 6.

Shulman, Alix Kates. "Dancing in the Revolution : Emma Goldman's Feminism". *Socialist Review* Mar-Apr. 1982 : 31-33.

Singh, Kushwant. "From Passion to Fantasy : Rev. of *Gods, Graves and Grandmother,*" by Namita Gokhale. *The Hindustan Times* 24 Sept. 1994 : 13.

———. "Genius of Shobha De". *The Hindustan Times* 9 May 1992 : 11.

Singh, Sushila. "Recent Trends in Feminist Thought : A Tour de Horizon". *Indian Women Novelists*. Ed. R. K. Dhawan. New Delhi : Prestige Books, 1990. 58-72.

Srivastava, Ramesh K. "Anita Desai at Work : An Interview". *Perspectives on Anita Desai*. Ed. Ramesh K. Srivastava. Ghaziabad : Vimal Prakashan, 1984. 210-213.

Stanton, Donna. C. and others. "Books That Changed Our Lives". *Women's Studies Quarterly* 19.3 - 4 (Fall/Winter 1991) : 8-29.

Stimpson, Catherine. R. and others. "Sexual Politics". *Women's Studies Quarterly* 19.3-4 (Fall/Winter 1991) : 30-40.

Subbu, Lalita. "Only An Enema!" Rev. of *Paro : Dreams of Passion*, Namita Gokhale. *Indian Literary Review* 48.2 (April 1986) : 87-91.

Thurow, Lester C " A Surge in Inequality". *Scientific American* 256.5 (May 1987) : 26.

Trehan, Madhu and Sunil Sethi. "A Time for Reckoning". *India Today* 15 August 1980 : 32-22.

Trilling, Diana. "The Liberated Heroine". *Partisan Review* 4 (1978) : 510-517.

Uma, Alladi. "I HAVE HAD MY VISION : Virginia Woolf's *To the Lighthouse* and Anita Desai's *Where Shall We go This Summer?*". *The Literary Criterion* 22.3 (1987) : 73-77.

Weir, AnnLowry. "The Illusions of Maya : Feminine Consiousness in Anita Desai's *Cry. The Peacock*". *Journal of South Asian Literature* 16.2 (Summer/Fall 1981) : 1-4.

Williams, H. M. "Victims and Virgins : Some characters in Markandaya's Novels". *Perspectives on Kamala Markandaya*. Calcutta : Writers Workshop, 1976. 24-29.

INDEX

'Aberration', 19, 21, 82, 85, 90, 99, 101, 109, 119, 120, 122, 128, 129
A Doll's House, 19
A Handful of Rice, 26, 27, 40, 41, 42, 43, 44, 45, 46
A Literature of Their Own, 14
Asnani, 65
Austen, Jane, 26

Beauvior, Simone de, 7, 8, 9
Belliappa, Meena, 3
Bhattacharya, Bhabani, 4
Bronte, Emily, 14

Chandra, Subhash, 89, 128
Clear Light of Day, 50, 51, 52, 71, 73, 75, 76, 78
Cry, The Peacock, 52, 53, 54, 55, 56, 57, 58, 59, 60, 61, 77
Communist Manifesto, 10, 16

Das, Kamala, 1
De, Shobha, 2, 3, 4, 21, 22, 81, 82, 90, 93, 95, 101, 109, 120, 121, 123, 126, 127, 128, 130
Defoe, Daniel, 5, 109
Desai, Anita, 3, 4, 18, 20, 21, 22, 49, 50, 51, 52, 76, 78, 81, 82, 86, 119, 129, 130

Engels, 7, 10, 17

Fanon, 14
Faustus, 12
Fire On the Mountain, 52, 66, 67, 68, 69, 70, 71, 77
Firestone, Shulamith, 11, 12, 65
Friedan, Betty, 7, 8, 13

Garg, Ajta, 16
Geetha, P., 24, 25, 34, 45, 46
Gods, Graves and Grandmother, 4, 112, 113, 114, 115, 116, 117, 118
Gokhale, Namita, 3, 4, 21, 22, 81, 82, 101, 120, 121, 123, 130
Gorrez, Christine, 131
Goyal, Bhagwat, 32, 33, 34
Greer, Germain, 7, 8
Gubar, Susan, 14

Heiburn, 26
Homer, 19, 20
Hussein, Rokeya, 14

Ibsen, 19

The Iliad, 19, 20

Jain, Jasbir, 50, 76, 130
Jane Eyre, 14
Jhabhwala, Ruth Prawar, 4
Juneja, Renu, 51

Karkaria, Bachi, J., 126
Khanna, S. M., 71
Krishnaswamy, Shantha, 4, 25, 26, 45, 46, 51

Lacan, Jaquest, 9
Larson, Charles, R..., 40

Mahle, H. S., 31
Mailer, Norman, 14
Markandaya, Kamala, 3, 4, 18, 19, 24, 25, 26, 27, 34, 35, 39, 41, 45, 46, 81, 82, 84, 86, 119, 120
Marx, Karl, 7, 10, 17
Mill, John Stuart, 12, 13
Miller, Henry, 14
Millet, Kate, 9, 14, 112
Mitchell Guliet, 11
Moll Flanders, 5, 109, 110, 111, 112, 113, 114, 115, 116, 117, 118, 129,
'Moll Flanders Syndrome' 19, 109, 112, 129
Murdoch, 26
My Story, 1

Narayan, R. K., 4
Nectar-in-a-Sieve, 26, 27, 28, 29, 30, 31, 32, 39, 40, 43, 44, 45, 46
'New Woman' 1, 2, 3, 17, 18, 21, 26, 33, 36, 52, 58, 60, 61, 66, 70, 76, 77, 78, 79, 81, 82, 111, 119, 120, 121, 122, 123, 124, 125, 126, 127, 129, 130

Parasuram, Laxmi, 67
Paro : Dreams-of-Passion, 101, 102, 103, 104, 105, 106, 107, 108
Poovaya, Nimmie, 64
Pritam, Amrita, 1

Ram, Atma, 49
Rao, C. Vimala, 3
Rao, K. S. Narayan, 45
Rao, Raja, 4
Raseedi Ticket, 1
Rossenwasser, Ruth K., 69

Sandra, Gilbert, 14
Sexual Politics, 9
Shriwadkar, Meena, 3
Showalter, Elaine, 14, 15, 65
Shulman, Alix Kates, 6
Socialite Evenings, 82, 83, 84, 85, 86, 87, 88, 89, 90, 96, 98, 104
Some Inner Fury, 25
Spencer, Sharon, 24
Srivastava, R. K., 49, 50, 51
Starry Nights, 82, 90, 91, 92, 93
Strange Obsession, 82
Sultry Days, 82, 93, 94, 95, 96, 97, 98, 99, 100, 120, 123
The Divided Mind : Studies in Defore and Richardson, 112
The Second Sex, 7
The Subjection of Women, 13

Thurow, 16
Trilling, Diana, 26, 35, 40
Two Virgins, 27, 34, 35, 37, 38, 39, 40, 45, 84, 85

Uncertain Liaisons, 126, 127

Vaid, Suresh, 112
Vindication of the Rights of Women, 12

Wadkar, Hansa, 1
Where-Shall-We-Go-This-Summer-? 52, 61, 63, 64, 65, 66, 74, 77
Williams, H. M., 24
Wollstonecraft, Mary, 12